# Praise for

# *Discovering Execution*

"OMG…. that is the thought that kept coming to me as I read this really engaging book. Execution and generating results are topics that we all deal with in business. In *Discovering Execution* these topics haves been served up in a unique, powerful and refreshing way. Language, commitment and systems are all dissected and translated in ways that will improve one's ability to execute as well as an organizations ability to create a culture of performance. I can hardly wait to be able to share this book and work to implement its ideas with my clients and leadership groups. Kudos to the authors for the contribution and insights this book provides and thanks for writing this book."

*Bruce Hodes, CMI Head Coach, Author, Speaker*

"Those who hire need to be convinced that you deliver, and that they would want to repeat the experience. Miles Kierson and Gary Tomlinson focus their extensive corporate experience on your relationship to requests, promises and follow-through in this profoundly simple book, to give you the tools to achieve what you're committed to, within a trustworthy environment. My relationship to my promises transformed on reading this book. Thank you!"

**Christopher Jones-Warner, Chartered FCSI, teacher of team communication and leadership**

"Execution is not as simple as doing what needs to be done. At its core, execution is a methodology fueled by the momentum to get done that which deserves to be achieved. *Discovering Execution* is a powerful and practical approach that challenges beliefs and biases about execution. Kierson and Tomlinson invite you to consider the science that drives meaningful actions and the performance-based outcomes that are realized when execution becomes a competency."

**Olalah Njenga, CEO, YellowWood Group**

"Learning the difference between action and execution from chapter 1 in paradigm shifting and when implemented creates value in you as a leader and certainly value in any business. This book condenses so many powerful and value releasing concepts that have been transformational to me as a leader."

**Christopher Morin, Executive Vice President, The Reserve Group**

"A decision is action starting to happen, and execution is action already yielding results. *Discovering Execution* points the way toward more focused and accountable actions that yield better results, in any setting. Kierson and Tomlinson are convincing— join them on the journey they describe and improve your organizational competence."

**Harry Hutson, Former executive at Cummins, Avery Dennison, Global Knowledge, and Devon Energy; consultant and author of** *Navigating an Organizational Crisis: When Leadership Matters Most*

"Dwight D. Eisenhower had a famous saying, 'The plan is nothing, planning is everything.' He was only partially right, because execution is really everything. In this book, authors Miles Kierson and Gary Tomlinson uncover the elements of execution. You'll learn about strategy, planning, engaging, and implementation in *Discovering Execution*. I highly encourage you to read this book and get on the journey to mastering execution to take your career and your business to the next level."

**Stan Phelps, Author, Forbes Contributor, IBM Futurist, TEDx Speaker, and CEO of PurpleGoldfish.com**

"If you want academic theory and surface platitudes, this book is not for you. If you are searching for practical knowledge and specific guidance to address an often ignored yet critical aspect of successfully driving and growing an organization, *Discovering Execution – The Key to High Performance Organizations* will be a valuable book for you. This is a must read for any business person."

**Gary Palin, Founder of SEEC and Professor of Entrepreneurship at Southern Maine University**

"After having trained over 100,000 businesses and corporations over the last thirty-five years, I get lots of requests for business book testimonials. Nothing pleased me more than reading Kierson's and Tomlinson's book *Discovering Execution.* Anyone who is looking to improve and accomplish results for their company or business needs to take a serious look at the basic principles presented in this book. Each chapter is packed with simple, easy-to-follow guidelines for growing their business and getting better results.

"While the idea of execution seems basic and obvious, *Discovering Execution* proves that thinking critically about execution is necessary to improve oneself or business. Miles and Gary effectively lay out the keys to execution and explain why the steps are important. Mastering execution can seem like a daunting feat, but *Discovering Execution* demonstrates it is through discovery, direction and commitment."

**Brian Azar, Coach, Sales Dr. and Author of**
*Your Successful Sales Career*

"I have known Gary Tomlinson and have had him address CEOs in my CEO peer groups. He is very passionate regarding execution and articulates it very well in both his presentations and this book. I have the opportunity to interface with many CEOs in my peer groups each month. I try to emphasize focus, transparency and accountability within their organizations. This book, with its clear definition and examples of execution, supports these objectives and provides a path to executing upon those things determined to be the most important in achieving greater success."

**Ray Watson Vistage Chair, Central Florida**

"Since 2013 Gary Tomlinson has helped me to discover execution through our twice monthly calls and holding me accountable as my "Chief Execution Officer". Although I first learned about Execution Management in 2001 as an original KeyneLink user, I did not understand the properties of execution or the Execution Cycle. Kierson and Tomlinson have unlocked the potential in my business by starting me on the journey to mastery of execution and will do the same for any leader that accepts their invitation to discover execution."

**Thomas H. Willingham, President, The Hampton Group**

# Discovering Execution:

## The Key to High Performance Organizations

# Discovering Execution:

## The Key to High Performance Organizations

Miles Kierson and Gary Tomlinson

ISBN 10: 1-944662-09-7

ISBN 13: 978-1-944662-09-7

Realization Press Publishing date: 11/07/2016


Cover Design by Rob Whatley, 1st Choice Grafix

# Dedication

This book is dedicated to our clients, past, present and future, including everyone from the executives to the front line employees who have made a contribution to us and the writing of this book.

*Kierson & Tomlinson*

# *Contents*

# Acknowledgements

Seeing our work's passion captured between the covers of a book is an experience that is humbling. Doubly so when you realize it could never have been done alone. *"Discovering Execution – The Key to High Performance Organizations"* is filled with the collective wisdom of our teachers, mentors, advisors, colleagues, and clients as well as our own experiences over the past several decades. We're grateful to all of them for their contributions. It may go without saying – without them, no discovery and no book.

Although there are too many to mention by name, there are three people whom we want to acknowledge and thank for their invaluable contribution to this work. They are:

**Wayne Nelsen**, founder and president of Keyne Insight for his generosity and partnership over the years, for his demonstrating the spirit of a learning collaboration, and for his being a mentor, a coach, and a friend.

**Rob Whatley**, founder and president of 1st Choice Grafix for his time and patience in designing the graphics, the book's cover, and all of the support materials that have gone into this endeavor.

**Drew Becker**, publisher and president of Realization Press for his guidance, wisdom, and labor in getting *Discovering Execution* published.

And finally, no *thank you* would seem adequate for all that our families have done to support us, but we'll thank them anyway.

# Foreword by Wayne Nelsen

When Miles and Gary asked me to review the manuscript and write the foreword for "Discovering Execution", I was honored to do so, having worked with them both for many years. I have to admit, though, I thought I would be quickly perusing the host of execution management concepts and processes that the three of us had explored and refined together over the past decade. What I found when I began reading this book was so much more than I had expected.

As I read, I became more and more excited about how they had approached a very complex subject. This was not another normal high-level process-oriented "how-to" book, or even another book on why you need to manage execution that fails to answer the most important question of exactly how execution ought to be managed. In this book, Miles and Gary get down to the very core of execution, to what they've termed the "molecular" level. After reading it, I began to understand it at an even deeper level than I ever had before, and I've been involved with execution management myself for over seventeen years. I kept thinking of issues happening with my current clients and how this explains the gaps they are experiencing. It's funny how the little things make such a big difference in our understanding and performance.

This is a powerful book that tackles an incredibly important subject.

I firmly believe that the lack of execution is the biggest issue facing organizations today. Poor performance in organizations is not due to lack of ideas or plans; it's due to poor execution. Statistics bear this out. Less than twenty percent of organizations actually achieve their strategic plans.

It is evident that most leaders do not understand the concepts involved with managing execution. When plans fail, they talk of issues with accountability, employee engagement, poor communication, lack of alignment, conflicting priorities, etc. These are all symptoms of poor execution. Because they don't understand execution, leaders are left to chase the symptoms. They don't know what they don't know. If you don't clearly identify the problem, you can't solve it in a sustainable way.

Once I started to study the issues surrounding execution, it became apparent that execution is most definitely not intuitive. Becoming a manager or leader doesn't make you good at execution any more than having a child makes you a great parent. It must be learned, understood, practiced and refined. I have found that much of what is done in organizations is contrary to great execution.

So what exactly is execution?

The definition my partner Kelly and I coined years ago to

anchor it for our work is this: Execution is clarifying, deploying and achieving organizational initiatives. Execution picks up where strategic planning and operational planning leave off. It ensures the entire organization is fully aligned with the operational plan and provides the structure needed to manage the accomplishment of the goals and tasks necessary to achieve the organizational initiatives.

There are many important building blocks that make up the concept of execution. Miles and Gary illuminate this in a way that is both practical and useful immediately.

Unexpectedly, I learned a lot from this book.

Why was I so surprised by how much I learned? After all, I've been studying and refining this subject for a long time. I have spent the last seventeen years deeply immersed in the subject of execution management.

My partner Kelly and I began developing our approach to execution management in 1999 after a particularly frustrating meeting with an aerospace client of ours. We had worked with them on their strategic plan a few years earlier and had just facilitated a meeting to review progress and "lessons learned". It was obvious that they had not made much progress even though everyone agreed that they had a solid plan. The execution had failed miserably. There were a lot of excuses and some finger pointing but no real definitive answers. At one point in the meeting I had gone up to the white board and erased the words "lessons learned" and replaced them with "lessons collected"; it seemed a much more appropriate description.

This certainly wasn't the first time we had experienced a company falling short of plan, but somehow this one seemed different. This one really struck a nerve with me. We really needed a better process for managing the communication and execution of these plans.

Kelly and I sat at dinner that night and began tossing around ideas for a new approach without making much real progress.

As fate would have it, two days later I was meeting with Randy, the president of a large courier company that had engaged us to help restructure his leadership team and conduct a lengthy leadership development program for his very inexperienced management staff. He was frustrated with the company's performance and asked if I would help redesign their performance appraisal process, thinking that would help to address the issues. I don't believe in performance appraisals and had no intention of helping to design a process that I still believe is based on a flawed premise.

However, as Randy and I talked further about his frustration, it soon became apparent that it was the lack of execution by his staff that he was really concerned with. I told him about the conversation Kelly and I had engaged in over dinner. Once we had connected the dots we both became very excited about designing an effective process for execution management.

I left his office at 7:00 pm on a Thursday evening and committed to him that we would develop a new program in time to roll it out at his monthly all-company meeting the following Monday morning. I was really excited about tackling this project and my excitement had gotten the better of me. When I got back to the office and relayed the conversation to Kelly, she let me know in her subtle but rather forceful way just how ridiculous this commitment was. As she quickly made clear to me, we now had three days to design a comprehensive new system from scratch that neither of us was clear about and with no time to do any real research. Remember, this was 1999; the internet had not really exploded onto the scene yet. She was not very happy over the next few days...

It did get better from there, though. We did in fact complete the project with a paper based process that turned out to be the rudimentary beginnings of KeyneLink, our current execution management process and KeyneLinkweb, its supporting software.

This was the beginning of an amazing journey for us. The more we discovered and learned about execution, the more interested we became. The journey became so intriguing and so consuming that in 2003 we restructured our entire consulting practice to focus exclusively on execution management. Since that time, which now seems so long ago, we have worked with hundreds of clients and certified scores of consultants in our KeyneLink execution management process. We are continually developing, testing and refining our processes.

For several years, Miles, Gary and I had a two-hour conference call twice a month in which we would explore our concepts, ideas and the results our clients were achieving. I remember one specific call in which Miles posited, "You know, we've been talking about this as execution management and I don't think that's big enough. I think this is really about execution mastery. We all are getting better and better at this each year and I don't see a defined end to this journey." That statement changed all of us and how we approached our work. Mastery is a journey without a defined or limiting end point – we grow, learn and further develop each year. You are invited to join us on this journey.

As you progress through this book, I hope you will read every word. It's not a long book, but it is a very important book.

I'm excited for you. You are about to embark on your own exciting journey, and as you learn more, I hope what you learned becomes part of the journey for all of us.

Wayne Nelsen
President and Founder
Keyne Insight, Inc.
The Keyne Institute for Execution Mastery

# *Your Invitation*

It can be said that every individual and every organization executes, and whether it is done well or not so well makes all the difference in terms of the outcome.

Everything you do that is purposeful takes execution. It takes execution to create a strategy. It takes execution to implement a strategy. It takes execution to do all of the day-to-day activities one does in their organization. Execution includes planning, engaging the organization, and implementing. It's all execution.

But here's the dilemma. If all we do is execute, then why don't we really focus on our ability to be good at it? Why doesn't every single leader have execution as the number one skill to excel in? More importantly, when are we going to discover execution?

Consider what it would be like in your organization if you had a real competency in execution. Not just that you were okay at it, but that you were great at it. What would there be to gain? The answer is everything.

Who wouldn't want their organization to have a competency in execution? Most executives and managers want something that takes execution to accomplish – they want to increase sales, they want to reduce errors in manufacturing, they want to get lean, they want to maximize profits, etc. You can get better at anything if you learn to get better at execution. By getting better at execution, you'll be better at executing more sales, higher production, less waste, stronger financials, etc.

Getting better at execution is the solution to getting better at everything.

The purpose of this book is to invite you to discover execution and then take on the mastery of execution, and to commit yourself to that journey. Keep in mind we're making an invitation to you to take on the mastery of execution, no matter what you do for work, regardless of the size of your organization and regardless of where you are in the hierarchy of that organization. If you're a CEO, consider this an invitation for you to take this on as the whole of your enterprise. If you're a leader of a division of a company, take it on for that division. If you're a manager or a team leader, take it on for your team. If you're an individual employee, take it on for yourself (you will positively impact the people around you).

The Age of Execution is Upon Us! You're invited!

# Preface:

# Why You Need to Discover Execution

"*The real voyage of discovery consists not in seeking new landscapes but in having new eyes.*"

Marcel Proust

We, the authors, had been focusing on execution in organizations for about 10 years before we first met and started collaborating on developing processes, adopting systems, and thinking together for our clients' benefit. A few years ago, we found ourselves asking the questions we asked in "Your Invitation":

> *"If all we do is execute, then why don't we really focus on our ability to be good at it? Why doesn't every single leader have execution as the number one skill to excel in? More importantly, when are we going to discover execution?"*

By then, it was very clear to us that (1) when we are doing anything we are executing; (2) we can improve upon our ability to execute; and (3) as we improved, we saw we could get better at everything. We were asking the questions above because too often when we were speaking with executives about execution, we would get blank stares, which to us seemed to be indications that something was missing in our conversations.

**What was missing?**

And then it struck us: Execution is so "everywhere" that people often don't pay any attention to it. They know what the word means...sort of. It's getting things done. You decide what you're going to do, and then you execute. We hear it from sports coaches, especially team sports. "We know what we have to do; we just have to execute." Here's a quote from a public company's third quarter report that we just heard recently:

> *"We executed well this year. We did what we wanted to do. We improved our profits."*

They did improve their profits. They did execute well, at least in that regard. But if you really wanted to explore it to determine what they did, if you went back with them over their year, what would you find? The odds are they had a better approach, a better strategy than the one they had before. Maybe as a company they focused more on profitability, or reducing costs, or working harder. Maybe they had new managers that were better at overseeing what was being spent versus what revenues were coming in. Maybe the market changed for the better.

Not to take anything away from them – because they did what they did, and it was positive – but do they have the ability to duplicate it, to even improve upon it; to methodically go about continuing what they did but have an even better year this year? And then again next year and the year after and so on?

**Asked another way…**

… Did they get better at execution? Did they even focus on execution? If they did, what have they learned as an organization about executing? What are the principles of execution, that if they improved in those, they would be better at everything?

And here's our key question, the one that will make all the difference: Have they discovered execution?

"Well, wait a minute," you might be protesting, "who are you that you can ask that question? Everybody knows what execution is. You can't discover what everybody already knows!"

**Yes you can, and you must!**

Sometimes, *humanity has to discover what "everybody already knows" because if we don't, we're not seeing what's right in front of us.*

We're two people who discovered execution. Actually, we're two people who discovered that execution needs to be discovered. People don't have much interest in learning how to improve at what isn't yet discovered.

*Execution* is analogous to air. Do you know what air is? Yes, of course, we all know what air is. It is that mostly invisible stuff that we breathe. It is oxygen and other gases.

**What is air?**

Wikipedia says;

*"Air is the Earth's atmosphere. Air around us is a mixture of many gases and dust particles. It is the clear gas in which living things live and breathe. It has an indefinite shape and volume. It has no color or smell. It has mass and weight. It is a matter as it has mass and weight. Air creates atmospheric pressure. There is no air in the vacuum and cosmos.*

*"Air is a mixture of about 78% nitrogen, 21% oxygen, 0.9% argon, 0.04% carbon dioxide, and very small amounts of other gases. There is an average of about 1% water vapour."*

Air is matter. If we could roll back the clocks, though, we would find that there was a time when air was *nothing*. There was only the space between objects. It was not only invisible; it *wasn't anything.* Science hadn't discerned oxygen or nitrogen or any of the other gases. They didn't exist. Air was air and air was nothing. It was everywhere and it was invisible and it was nothing.

And then somebody came along and said, "Wait a minute, air is something. It has stuff in it. It is a thing. It is matter. If we knew what that stuff in it was, we could make the air better, cleaner. We could know how to affect the air differently so it was healthier for us." And so on.

### Execution is like air

Execution is like air, but only in that it, too, is everywhere and invisible. It is so ubiquitous in our organizational language that we never realized that execution is *something* just like air is *something*. Execution describes and proscribes a series of activities that is aimed at producing a specific result or at getting us to a specific place.

Execution has properties and principles. If you study and practice these properties and principles, you can learn how to get better and better at execution. Once you can say, "I get it! There is such a thing as execution!", the possibility exists that you could take it up, you could learn about it, you could study it, you could learn practices that would help you to get better and better at it. However, if you haven't said that, if you haven't discovered it, what's the likelihood that you can get better at it?

The analogy of execution to air stops there, though. For example, one way execution is unlike air is that when air is lacking, you know it. Stick your head in a tub of water and see how long it takes to notice that the air is seriously lacking. Pretty quickly, you'd miss it so badly that you'd do anything to get it. Well, what do organizations do when execution is seriously lacking? Ironically, here's the answer: they do everything else they can think of but they never take on execution! Why? *Because they haven't discovered execution.* They don't know it exists except as a word. It never occurs to them *that execution is something they can take on and get better at!*

**What this book is meant to be**

This book is meant to be your vehicle for discovering execution. Maybe this preface has helped move you along. Our invitation to you is actually three-fold:

1. We invite you to discover execution.

2. We invite you to learn some practices that will help you improve your individual and organizational ability to execute.

3. We invite you to get on board for the journey to the mastery of execution – the most valuable organizational and personal competency you can have.

The Age of Execution is upon us! You are welcome to it!

**How to read this book**

When we began writing this book, we had between us many years of consulting and coaching with organizations ranging in size from very large to very small. We also each started, built, and ran our own enterprises; plus, we've been senior executives in other companies and have served on boards of directors. We were both certified in the same execution management system that we use with our clients. And for several years we were senior advisers to the president and founder of that company. The three of us participated in bi-weekly telephone calls discussing our experiences in using this execution management system with our clients and, in general, the principles and practices of learning to execute more effectively. All three of us learned a tremendous amount during that period.

In addition, we learned a lot writing this book, way more than we would have ever imagined. In a way, the book itself was a third co-author of itself. In fact, in the beginning, we were going to call the book *The Mastery of Execution* but early on, the book re-named itself to *Discovering Execution*. We are sharing this with you because we believe that this book is very rich in introducing a new and deeper understanding of execution. If you read it like we wrote it – from beginning to end – you'll gain tremendously as a result, whether you accept our invitation to get on the journey to mastery of execution or not. But the journey is 10,000 times more enriching than the book, so we highly recommend you remain open to the possibility that you'll take it on.

We suggest that you read it from beginning to end. Learn it in order and take some time with it. Do what you can to learn along with us. There are numerous gems in here – things we learned either working with clients in our many discussions about execution, in working with past and current clients, or just in the process of writing this book. Gems we learned that you won't have heard elsewhere, and are worth exploring.

Each chapter has a title which is both its theme and an essential element for learning to execute. We put it in an order that attempts to build onto each other. Chapter 5, for example, won't have much meaning if you haven't read chapters 1, 2, 3, and 4. After you've read it through once, if you want to go back to individual chapters, go ahead and do that. But we suggest the first reading be done in order.

Each chapter also has a summary, which will reinforce what you just read and serve as a quick reminder of what is in the chapter. We originally were thinking of this as a manual, but then we purposely didn't write it in that format. This book is an invitation to begin the journey to mastery of execution, a process in itself for discovering execution. You can't take on the mastery of something that isn't yet really discovered.

We decided to use the personal pronoun *we*, even when telling a story that only one of us actually experienced. We did this because we decided we didn't want this to be about us as individuals, and we didn't think it mattered to you if it was Gary or Miles who was reporting an actual event. We are individuals who met in 2010 and discovered that we complement each other nicely in our work. We have enormous respect each for each other's capabilities, and share a passion for learning and (as it turns out) exploring and discovering.

We're very grateful to our past and present clients. Please don't be disturbed if you only met one of us and we're talking about your organization as if there was a "we" there, one of which has a name you don't recognize.

Fasten your seat belts and enjoy the ride!

*"A philosophy of life: I'm an adventurer, looking for treasure."*

Paulo Coelho, 21st century Brazilian writer

# ❦ *Chapter 1* ❧

# What Is Execution?

*"I always love that phrase, 'Oh, this is a good idea, but it's execution dependent.' As if anything in life is not execution dependent. Breathing is execution-dependent."*

Ted Sarandos, Chief Content Officer, Netflix

*Kierson & Tomlinson*

## Beginning at ground zero

One of the most important points we've learned as consultants, trainers, and public speakers in working with teams and other groups is that you have to define and re-define everything. If you don't include this important step, you're going to spend a lot of time explaining the very meaning of the concept or topic you're tackling. In the end, if you and your team haven't reached a mutual understanding of the topic, the result or conclusion of your meeting is going to unravel and – as we all know – ideas made without a firm foundation are going to crumble.

Related to this need for common understanding is blending the need for authority of the matter with practicality. In other words, we can go to the dictionary (now accessible in seconds on our computers and numerous devices), which is considered to be the "final word". Google gives us this when the definition of execution is searched:

1. *the carrying out or putting into effect of a plan, order, or course of action.*
2. *the carrying out of a sentence of death on a condemned person.*

For now, we'll ignore the second meaning above. Looking at the first one, we now know what execution is, right? No. We know the "official" meaning of it – actually an official meaning of it, since there are numerous dictionaries with varied definitions. The problem is that although we consider the dictionary the authority (how else would you settle disagreements in Scrabble?); it is not really the final word. It is not a sacred truth; it is a societal standard developed with much input and intelligence which serves as a temporary statement of what a word means. Does it help you to improve your ability to execute? Not much, if at all.

We're going into some detail in this discussion about definitions because we've found that sometimes we have to develop our own statements about what a word means that go beyond the dictionary definitions. We do this not because we disagree with the accepted definitions but because we need a common understanding of our use of the word, and we shape what we mean with the word's practicality in mind. We're offering that all of us will benefit if we can agree for at least a moment on one meaning for the word or phrase that we're using in our quest for improvement – in this case, execution mastery.

*Ground zero* here refers to our recommendation that whatever you think *execution* is, whatever you think you know what it is, you need to let it go, place it in your mind in a kind of drawer that doesn't eliminate it but puts it where you can find it later. Remember, the purpose of this is to have you *discover execution*, and if you're going to discover it you must at least temporarily let go of what you think it is.

**Our Proposed Usage of the Word Execution**

As a start, the dictionary definition is pretty good – "*the carrying out or putting into effect of a plan, order, or course of action.*" It does give us an idea of what execution is. It is limited, though, because it simply is not enough to shed any light on the depth and breadth of what the word represents. Actually, most people who read that definition will say "Yes, that is what I thought it was."

In 2002, Larry Bossidy, an experienced and successful CEO of large publicly-traded companies, and Ram Charan, a respected and knowledgeable author of business books, had published what turned out to be one of the most well-read business books of the decade, *Execution: The Discipline of Getting Things Done* (well worth reading, in our opinion). The title serves as a definition that is useful, "the discipline of getting things done". However, in their words, it is more than that:

> *"Execution is not just something that does or doesn't get done. Execution is a set of behaviors and techniques that companies master in order to have competitive advantage."*

**And then they add:**

> *"It is a discipline of its own. In big companies and small ones, it is the critical discipline for success now."*

It is a discipline of its own, which is why we've been emphasizing that one needs to discover execution. If you don't discover execution as a discipline of its own, you won't take it on. You'll examine your organization's structure, you'll re-engineer, you'll have town hall meetings and talk about accountability – all of which are worthy endeavors that will yield some results. But, again, will you have improved your ability to execute?

It is worth reviving an old joke:

*Upon turning her CEO duties over to her successor, she said to the new CEO, "In your top desk drawer, there are three envelopes, numbered one, two, and three. If you find yourself at wit's end regarding the company's progress, open and read the instructions in the first envelope. If, at a later time, you are in similar dire straits, go to the second envelope. And, if you find yourself in the same circumstances a third time, go to the third envelope. Good luck and goodbye."*

*Some months went by and the new CEO found himself in a quandary beyond his experience in terms of what to do, and he opened the first envelope. The note inside said, "Implement lean principles." He thought this was perfect advice, and immediately began a project to implement lean principles across his company. Waste was eliminated and the company emerged from its lull and showed life. All was good.*

*But it didn't solve all of their problems, and the CEO found himself again going to the envelopes in his drawer. The note inside the second envelope said, "Engage your employees so everyone has line of sight to the vision." This sounded like a good idea, and the CEO put a team together who came up with a year-long plan for accomplishing this. At the end of the year, the employees were well versed in the vision and knew how their job impacted the fulfillment of that vision.*

*Some more time passed; the excitement grew dim. The CEO went to the drawer for a third time, and the note said: "Time to write three new notes, put them in envelopes, and leave them for your successor."*

We want to only put one envelope in your desk drawer. The note would read: "Take on the journey to mastery of execution." If you get on that journey there is no need for more envelopes. Execution is everything you do. That's what execution is – everything you do. If this is true, if execution is everything that you do, and you got better at execution, what could you get better at? Think about it; actually answer the question. What could you get better at?

If you said, "I could get better at everything", you get an "A". That's right; you could get better at everything and anything. And if you could get better at anything, what would you want to achieve? We recommend you think about this question and answer it for yourself. If you do, you may take a giant step toward discovering execution.

Execution, as we have stated, is everything that you do, but we want to add that it is everything you do in order to fulfill the purpose of your activity. If you are an athlete, execution is in order to win the game, and ultimately to win the championship. If you are working in a company, it is in order for the company to be successful (as defined by that company's leadership). Execution, therefore, is everything you do, and this includes strategy, planning, engaging, and implementation. We are focusing in this book on the implementation part of execution.

## Who Executes?

We assert that who executes is the individual. People do things. Organizations do not do anything, therefore they do not execute. That being said, we sometimes speak as if they do, and it makes sense to do that. We say things like, "This Company is very good at execution", which we would legitimize, but in actuality an organization that can accomplish what it sets out to do has individuals who can execute and individuals who are good at managing execution (a form of executing in itself).

Let us emphasize this does not mean that teams and teamwork aren't essential and potent in taking on projects of all kinds including leading entire organizations. We'll temporarily leave the subject of teams to reiterate the point that *individuals execute.* Teams can be said to be a group of individuals who are working together to a common end, and each executes as harmoniously and collaboratively as they can to accomplish their desired results.

An individual's accountability in an organization is to execute in accord with their job responsibilities and toward fulfillment of their goals that contribute to the success of that organization. If you take this last statement to be true, then it can be simply stated as: *the focus of management is to help the individuals and teams be successful, and when they are, then the organization will be as successful as it can be.*

## Summary

To come to a working definition of execution, we start at ground zero, as much as we can. We assert that execution is a discipline of its own. Our short working definition of execution is that it is everything you do. Practically speaking, it is everything you do, and includes strategy, planning, engaging, and implementation. It is critical to keep in mind that in the end, it is individuals who execute.

# NOTES

_____

_____

_____

_____

_____

_____

_____

_____

_____

_____

_____

_____

_____

_____

_____

_____

_____

_____

_____

_____

_____

# NOTES

_____

_____

_____

_____

_____

_____

_____

_____

_____

_____

_____

_____

_____

_____

_____

_____

_____

_____

_____

_____

_____

_____

# ❧ *Chapter 2* ❧

# The Language of Execution:

## The Portal to the Journey to Mastery of Execution

*"But if thought corrupts language, language can also corrupt thought."*

George Orwell, *1984*

We were sitting with the CEO of a charitable organization headquartered in Chicago, not really feeling like we were getting anywhere with her, when she made a reference to some words used by Jim Collins in his book *Good to Great*. When we told her we were familiar with the phrase our conversation suddenly got very energetic and exciting. As it turns out, she did not become a client; but as we were leaving she gave us a copy of a little book that sparked a whole new way of thinking for us about execution.

The book was called *Good to Great in the Social Sectors* by Jim Collins, and it contained this line that hit us both like a thunderbolt:

> *"We need to jointly embrace a language of greatness."*

A language of greatness! This was a piece of the puzzle we were missing. What is the language of execution, and shouldn't it be filled with the language of greatness?

A great company can be defined as a company that performs consistently beyond expectations (and yes, is a great place to work, but we'll get to that later) – in other words, executes.

So there needs to be a language of execution that embraces greatness. Perhaps it would sound like Beethoven's Ninth Symphony, in our opinion one of the greatest musical compositions ever, and, we would add, heroic.

## How critical is language?

Does the language we use and how we use it make a difference at work? It not only makes a huge difference, for many of us it is what we do at work. What else do leaders, executives, managers,

and all white collar workers do but converse; that is, speak and listen? Yes, they read emails (a form of listening) and they write emails (a form of speaking); they think (sometimes speaking and sometimes listening); they "lead by example" (but how do they do that except by speaking and listening?); they point to the future (speaking); they make plans and set goals (speaking and listening); and so on.

Sometimes when people hear or read that all they do at work is speak and listen, their immediate reaction is to get upset or defensive and deny that this is true. At first it sounds like an insult or an accusation – "All you do at work is speak and listen!"

But, wait a minute! If all you do is speak and listen, then you are executing, right? For the most part, that is right. There are many people who physically do things at work (not counting walking to another office and sitting down and standing up). There are people who operate machinery and who fix things and who climb telephone poles and drive trucks. Yes, there are those people, and their work is execution, too, and at least as significant and honorable and useful as those who don't do those things. But the physical activity associated with work can be said to be a response to a conversation (which is part of what we call the execution cycle in the next chapter), and is surrounded by conversation and language in many forms.

Let's just conclude for now that speaking and listening is critical to work, in one form or another, and for many of us it is all we do. Where do we learn how to speak and listen purposefully and powerfully at work (or in any other milieu)? We learned how to talk from our parents, who also might have insisted we listen as well. But when did you study the effectiveness of language? Or how to listen? You might have been in a workshop that included an aspect of this, but did you ever really study it? And if you did, where did you study? As far as we know, it is not a subject in graduate schools and not an MBA requirement.

The point is, if speaking and listening is so critical, what is our skill and knowledge level? Read on.

## The Current Language of Execution

We listed a number of words and phrases which were closely identified and used often when speaking about execution, and we asked this question: What do people hear when these words are spoken? What is the unspoken implication in their minds about each of the words?

Below is a list that is a decent sampling of the most common words or phrases in the language of execution. As an experiment, take each word one at a time, say the word, and write down what your first reaction is when you heard the word. There is no right or wrong here, we're only asking for what reaction you have to the word – not what you think the word means, not what the good soldier in you says it means because you "already know" all the answers; rather, does it feel good to you or bad to you when you hear it? Does it have a negative or a positive connotation? What is your immediate reaction to it?

As an example, what is your initial reaction to the word pain? Does it feel good or bad? For most people, it feels bad. Does it make you aware of some part of your body that has some pain? Do you feel it in your gut when you hear the word? Do you wince?

Okay, here's the list. Do yourself a favor and don't just read the list and say you get it. Rather than just reading the list, spend some time with it and pay attention to what your initial reaction is to the word or phrase:

- *Execution*

Take a few seconds and notice your reaction or thought. Close your eyes for a moment if that helps. Remember, this takes some ability to observe yourself, not your "already established" interpretation of the word. Do the same with each of the following words.

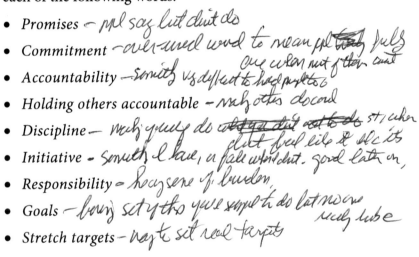

- *Promises* — ppl say but dont do
- *Commitment* — over-used word to mean pretty much. One when not often cant
- *Accountability* — Something vg difficult to hold ppl to
- *Holding others accountable* — makes others discord
- *Discipline* — makes yourself do what did not want to do stricter. But feel like I dic its
- *Initiative* — Something I have, a false word that. good lath on,
- *Responsibility* — heavy sense of burden,
- *Goals* — boring set of ths you're suppos'd to do but noone really lube
- *Stretch targets* — hay to set real targets

Generally, when we ask ten people about each of these words and phrases, we get negative reactions for anywhere from two to ten of them; positive reactions from none to three; and neutral (neither positive nor negative) from none to four or five.

Below are the typical negative responses we typically hear, but the samplings are not complete, so you can add your own to them:

- *Execution* – "Chop off heads"; "Kill"; "Something management is always trying to get us to do, but we can never seem to get it right enough for them."

- *Promises* – "Something your child asks you to do when she really wants you to mean what you say and doesn't trust you even after you've responded"; "Not a word we use much as adults"; "An empty word that, when used, doesn't guarantee anything."

- *Commitment* – "Something to be afraid of, like 'marriage' before you are married"; "What management will try and get you to do in order to manipulate you"; "Sent to an asylum."

- *Accountability* – "Something else management will beat me over the head with"; "It has a heaviness about it"; "Code for blame."

- *Holding other people accountable* – "Something you are supposed to do that nobody in this organization actually does"; "If you don't do something to their expectations, you will be in trouble"; "A way management thinks they can bully their way to getting you to do what they want you to do."

- *Discipline* – "Spanking or hitting you over your knuckles with a ruler"; "What will happen if you don't play the game the way they want you to play it"; "A sado-masochist's word"; "Something you have to do every day that you don't want to do."

- *Initiative* – "What they tell me I need to have to be

successful, but I don't have enough of "; "Something that if I just keep my head down, this too shall pass"; "Their latest 'good idea' that's only going to mean more work for me."

- *Responsibility* – "It's my fault"; "A burden of guilt"; "What they keep adding to my job that means more work and the same pay."

- *Goals* – "What I set for myself that nobody else cares about or supports"; "What is set for me that I don't care about but my job or my raise or both depend on it"; "Something I hope I will for once actually accomplish."

- *Stretch targets* – "A way for those above me to succeed and make bigger bonuses"; "Torture"; "A phrase that becomes popular every time a new consultant comes to town."

We didn't just make the above up – they are typical responses that people have to those words as they reported their responses to us. If you think about it, it's pretty dismal. The point here is that the words associated with execution often have a negative connotation, and unless this changes in our own minds and in the culture of our organizations, we/they are going to have a tough time being successful at execution. You may not have had the same negative reaction to these words, but we've done this enough times with enough people that we know it is a common issue.

When we listed each word on a sheet of paper and put small circles with colors next to each word – red meaning very negative, pink meaning a little negative, yellow meaning neutral, and white meaning positive – what it ending up looking like was a bouquet of roses that was dominated by red. If you think of the reactions that these colors represent, you have to conclude, as we did, something has to change.

Here's a fairly typical manager's speech to his/her direct reports:

> *"We are going to be better at execution; we are going to take the initiative to discipline ourselves, to be accountable and hold others accountable so we can reach our goals and achieve our initiatives."*

Guess what people are thinking when they hear this? Where did they check out – on the first sentence or the second? And you know this as well as we do – executives and managers make these kinds of speeches often. What the audience hears is something like this: *"I'm getting a lot of pressure so I'm going to lay it on you. I'm going to slap you around a lot in the name of getting results. And I want you to be excited about it."*

Let us be clear about two connected things: (1) not everybody has the same negative reaction to these words. For example, we don't anymore and many of our clients don't either; and (2) we are not necessarily advocating the invention of new words or even using different words, although we are not opposed to that either. What we are in favor of is re-thinking and re-establishing the positive connotations of these words in organizations.

We'll be addressing each one of the words in new ways as the book progresses. You might have a better way to re-state them than our way. Be clear that the mandate is to be responsible for the words you use in the name of execution if you want others in your organization to embrace execution or the journey to mastery of execution. Keep in mind we all would benefit from developing a language of greatness for mastering execution. And we pay dearly when we ignore how people react to the words we use.

## Summary

We need a language of greatness to have great companies. The language we use makes a difference. And it also makes a difference to learn how to speak and listen better in order to execute better. The current language of execution is, on the whole, loaded with negative connotations, and we have to begin to change all that. We need to have shared definitions around the current language of execution that is positive and encouraging.

*haven't shown this – just stated it.*

# NOTES

# NOTES

# Chapter 3

# The Execution Cycle

*"The most effective way to do it, is to do it."*

Amelia Earhart, American aviation pioneer

There is a certain cycle that is in operation many, many times a day in all of work and in every organization, and very few people are aware of it. Once you really understand what this cycle is, you'll begin to see it in action all around you and you'll wonder why you never knew this or never noticed it before. It may seem simple, and it is simple, but don't let its simplicity fool you. This is a very powerful language tool that, once learned, will greatly improve the likelihood that what people agree to do will be done, and done in the way that it was originally intended. In fact, if you learned just this one skill and practiced it steadfastly, you would considerably increase your "execution intelligence" and capability. If you committed yourself to it and spread it around to your team (or your whole company), you could transform the group's ability to work together, to implement strategy and other plans, and in general to accomplish what you set out to do – not just once but over and over again, getting better at it as you proceed.

Before we reveal the cycle itself, it needs a little background. We first learned about this in a workshop we participated in more than thirty years ago that was led by Fernando Flores, a fascinating and brilliant Chilean politician and engineer who holds a PHD from the Computer Science Department at Stanford. Flores spoke of *speech acts*, a linguistic term that includes *performatives*, which points to a class of words the speaking of which are the performance of the act. An example of a performative is the word *promise*. When you say "I promise (something)", you are performing/doing the act of promising. In contrast, if you say, for example, "I feel", or "I think", you are describing something, not performing it; you are not *feeling or thinking* by saying the words. If you say "I am going to the supermarket" it does not mean you are doing anything as a function of having said it, while "I promise I will go to the supermarket" is the promising. "*I promise*" is the act of promising something, while those other statements are merely the act of describing something.

Have we confused you? Don't get hung up on this – it's just background for what we call the *execution cycle*, and it's not essential for getting a glimpse of, and understanding, the cycle and its power. The nature of performatives is worth exploring further; although, it's not a topic we will tackle in this book. Keep it in mind, though, that there are words that are acts in themselves when spoken.

And please note: everything we express in this book is not simply something we heard someone else say and it sounded good. It may be something we heard from someone else but we learned from applying it to our client work plus we've added the spin we've put on it after years (and in most cases many years) of using it and honing it to make it useful. Just so you know, our typical spin is in order to bring it down to its simplest, most practical application. As William James has said:

> "*A great number of people think they are thinking when they are merely rearranging their prejudices.*"

Our prejudice at work is to make everything as simple and useful as it can be.

As we have already stated, the execution cycle is a language cycle, consisting of language acts. *Requests and promises* are two of those performative words we discussed above. A *request* is when you are asking someone to do something and a *promise* is when they say they're going to do it. It could be said all work is a series of requests and promises. Your job can be seen to be an implicit or explicit request or a series of requests to fulfill on what the job requires. Your acceptance of the job is a promise or series of promises as a response to the offer made by whoever hired you, whether it's a manager or a committee or a board of directors. If you do not fulfill on the job requirements, it stands to reason you have failed to keep your promises, and at some point if you cannot keep your promises, you ought to be given a different job or be let go. When you accept a position, it is typically implicit that you have promised to fulfill that position's requirements.

It may be helpful to think of a request/promise transaction as the atom of work. If you could take a microscope to the activity of work, you would find underneath all of the activity, all of the drama, all of the effort, all of the theory, all of the individual quirks – at the most basic level, work is an ongoing complex of requests and promises, an atonal symphony that manifests in the results you produce and in the results you don't produce. It is going on in the background, unnoticed and invisible to almost everybody.

If the atom of work is the dual unit of requests/promises, then the execution cycle is the molecule. It consists of somebody making a request, somebody saying they will do it and a follow through or fulfillment of the original request and promise.

Graphically, the cycle of execution can be represented like this on the following page:

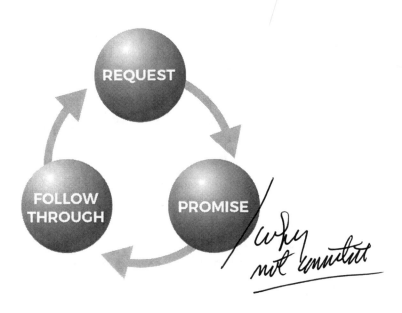

*why not consistent* (handwritten note)

The above model constitutes what we're saying is analogous in execution matters to the molecule in physics. Just like in physics, this is the molecule and in the language of execution, the cycle is the molecule which is represented as something like this:

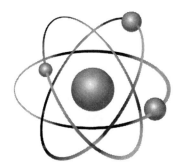

The cycle, in its basic form, goes like this:

A request is made. Someone promises to fulfill on that request and then follows through and completes it. For example, the CEO requests the CFO to prepare a particular report on a capital call by the middle of next month so it can be discussed at the board meeting, which is coming up the following month. She says she will, and then she does it, prints it out, and puts it on his desk. Or, a manager asks a welder to apply a spot weld on a piece of equipment so that it fixes a bothersome rattle; the welder agrees to do it. He does it and it fixes the rattle. These are examples of completed cycles. They're also examples of relatively clear requests and promises. They represent simple examples of the cycle in action.

## Requests and Promises

If we look deeper, we begin to understand there's more to it. In terms of execution, the problem is that most of these cycles are not so explicit and not so clear. In fact, we don't even know they exist. Often, there's not a clear request. Rather than "I request of you…" or even "Would you…", we often just say, "Do this". And even less clear is "I would like this report for the meeting" (which has many flaws, as you shall see, including the legitimate possibility that you could say, "Okay, thanks. It's good to know what you would like.").

The "more to it" that we mentioned above has to do with the requirements for effective cycles. An effective cycle is one that maximizes the likelihood of getting the wanted result. Effective execution cycles require effective requests, including who you are asking the promise from, what it is that you want, exactly when you want it, and in what form you want it. There are always *conditions of satisfaction*, which define what must happen so that you'll be satisfied you got what you wanted.

You might ask if this is too much, but think of the complexity in even very simple requests at work. For example; "Get me some water, please" rarely requires any other descriptors, because we all know what that means. It means drinking water in a glass in the next few minutes. We are used to that. There is some social norm assumed in that question. But think about it; someone could come back with a fire hose or a bucket of water.

At work, though, when you actually ask someone for something rather than order it from an "underling" (a demeaning word, in our opinion), we generally need much more specificity and clarity. "I want that report by Friday" sounds clear enough, but do you want it first thing Friday morning or by the end of the day? Would midnight be okay? And do you want it electronically or in hard copy on your desk?

We've heard the following complaint more times than you can count from executives and managers over the years: "I made it perfectly clear what I wanted, and he still screwed it up!" Really? Perfectly clear? Maybe it was perfectly clear to you, but obviously it wasn't perfectly clear to whomever you asked to do it.

Here are some of the ways the execution cycle is poorly carried out or not carried out at all in organizations:

- Requests are not made in the first place; rather, utterances which are more like orders without much clarity are emitted.

- Requests are made but the requestor didn't really care if it got done or not.

- Requests are made but are not clear.

- When requests are communicated, the promisor does not ask questions or ask enough questions of the requestor to make the request clear enough.

- There is a response from the promisor, but it is not a promise. "I'll try", "I'll do my best", and "Sure" are not promises.

- The promisor doesn't mean it. Associated with this, the promisor knows that the requestor won't follow up and therefore it doesn't matter.

- Nobody keeps all of their promises. Some people are good at keeping their promises, but not so good at informing the requestor when it is clear that they won't be able to keep the promise.

- Although nobody keeps all of their promises, most people will deny this because they think it's wrong to not keep their promises. This is not a moral issue. This is an effectiveness issue and an accountability issue.

- In many, if not most organizations, an order is g
  or a request is made and there just doesn't seem
  enough time or enough desire to actually talk about it,
  to be clear about it, and especially to hear whether the
  promisor can actually promise it and be able to deliver
  on that promise.

- Very few people follow up on promises made to them
  at work. Even fewer people hold others accountable
  for promises made. Rather, they collect judgments
  about people and make conclusions about their lack
  of accountability, but they put up with it. In a recent
  board meeting, a CEO admitted, "We have a culture
  that believes it is okay to not do what you said you
  were going to do if you have a good excuse."

The above is a sampling of what occurs, of the mischief
that gets created when there isn't any awareness of the need for
execution cycles to be effective and completed. Said with more
emphasis, *this is what happens! It is going on right now, today, in
your organization.*

There's so much more to know to begin to master this, but
you can begin to practice it, and, when you do, you and your
organization will benefit. Consider this: every day there are
dozens or hundreds or thousands of these cycles going on around
you, but they're very often unclear, unnoticed, and unfulfilled in
the manner that was needed. It affects everything – your ability
as an organization to execute, the success or failure of staff and
employees, the professional relationships that you have or don't
have with each other, and so on. This mish-mash of sloppy
transactions is like the "ghosts in the machine" – forces that are
there in the background having a huge impact on performance

while you're trying desperately to get better without taking into account what is going on.

Below is pretty close to how we envision the chaos in the background; or, said another way, *this represents what is going on in just about every organization:*

*Painting by Christoph Glarner*

We could write a manual for learning how to speak the language of execution and, in particular, the language of the execution cycle. That manual would be a couple of hundred pages or more. In our experience, it takes about a day of training to have a group of people experience the power of the cycle and learn how to do it successfully enough that they would be on a good learning track. You then need to have additional follow-up to reinforce and help boost their capability. They can learn it themselves, if they're willing, but a good coach will speed up the process immensely.

In our view, to maximize your journey to mastery of execution, you must to do four things:

- Make the commitment.

- Practice keeping your promises.

- Be aware of and practice shepherding the execution cycle through to completion.

- Adopt and use an execution management system.

## The Cost of the Incomplete Cycle

When the execution cycle is left incomplete, the cost to the organizational culture is very dear. Pick any reason why the cycle would be abandoned before it is completed and you can see what negative effects are left.

Typically, as we've alluded to before, a manager will say to someone, "I need the report we've been discussing by Friday". There is no request, nor is there a demand; there is only an implication. There is little specificity about the request and there is no promise. The odds are not good that it'll be done, done in time, or done the way the manager expected. She runs around on Friday and finds her employee, who has some excuse why it couldn't get done. She's frustrated and decides the employee is incompetent. She then gets someone else to do the report over the weekend. She gets it on Monday, but unfortunately she doesn't have sufficient enough time to prepare herself for the meeting for which she needed the report. The meeting doesn't go over very well. Her manager is angry at her now and he asks her what happened, and she blames it on the original employee who didn't get it done on Friday. Relationships are bruised and the story is a confirmation that "you can't count on people here."

That's just one example. Here's another. Every time someone makes a promise to you that doesn't get done and you don't follow up with them, guess what that person thinks? Quite often, they think to themselves, "I don't need to do what he says, because he won't remember anyway", or "he doesn't mean it."

We think of incomplete execution cycles as the ghosts in the machine because in subtle and not-so subtle forms they linger to haunt you and to feed the organizational culture with evidence that, in fact, things are as bad as we think they are.

**Summary**

There is a mostly unnoticed cycle that is going on many, many times a day in every organization. This execution cycle consists of a request, a promise, and a follow through. Since hardly anybody knows about this cycle, hidden in the "ether" of the organization there are likely an enormous multitude of uncompleted or partially completed cycles that contribute to our culture of less-than-masterful execution. We all need to replace these failures to execute with consistent success. Simply put, we need to take the execution cycle on, to be willing to learn it, and to be willing to practice it.

## NOTES

_____

_____

_____

_____

_____

_____

_____

_____

_____

_____

_____

_____

_____

_____

_____

_____

_____

_____

_____

_____

_____

_____

# Chapter 4

# Relationships at Work Matter

*"Entrepreneurs as 'soloist' will be replaced by orchestras playing a stronger, more credible tune."*

Steve Case, founder of America Online, from *The Third Wave*

For years, we'd been saying that relationships at work matter in one form or another. The leadership models we use with our clients are the building blocks for creating high performance organizations and teams, and at the base of those building blocks are *relationships*. The point here is that if you aren't producing the results you want, check out the relationships of the people involved in the execution related to the metric. We often found that until we came along, when managers weren't getting the results they wanted, the best they could do was to find someone to blame. Even sophisticated root cause analyses were often geared toward blaming someone for the failure. The old joke is: *"The purpose of the root cause analysis is to blame somebody else for what happened."*

We've tested this out. When asked, most executives will agree, or at least concede, that relationships are very important in their organizations, and after a little dialog, most will agree that relationships are the most important factor in producing results. Recently, when we searched for "relationships at work" on Amazon, there were 3,685 items on the list, but after the first few pages of items, most of them had nothing at all to do with that topic. For example we found books on peppermint oil, an anti-bark collar for dogs, and yoga mats. And even early book titles included one about playing the ukulele, another about overcoming sexual anxiety, and *The Work at Home Mom's Guidebook*. The relevant books were mostly zeroing in on problems and specific improvements at work that have to do with relationships. Only a few were really about relationships at work in general. After many conversations with each other and with our other colleagues as well as client executives – we came to two conclusions:

1.    There is very little known or written about relationships

at work in general (we haven't yet run into anybody who claims to really know a lot about relationships at work).

2. Even though many people will admit that relationships at work are important, they have little attention on them and mostly just hope that they all get along okay. In fact, when asked what it means to them that relationships at work are important, they mostly did some version of shrugging their shoulders.

## The purpose of relationships at work

We assert that the purpose of relationships at work is the success of the enterprise. We are all there to enhance the success of the company. As individuals, our own agenda may be something like getting paid and advancing our career. But if you think about it beyond yourself and your own personal agenda, you'll come up with the same conclusion we did. You are there to help the company be successful, and if that's the case, then the purpose of your relationships at work is to help each other further the success of the company.

Outside of work, what's the purpose of your relationships? What's the purpose of your friendships, for example? If you ask yourself that last question, you might find it more difficult to answer, because there are likely a myriad of purposes. The purpose of a relationship with a friend may be to have someone to talk to, to drink a beer with, to tell stories to, to have someone who will give you sympathy, to have someone just to hang out with, to have someone you trust to help you when you're in need. Of course, there is nothing wrong with any of that; we're simply pointing out the difference between work relationships and other social relationships.

We've found that this idea – *that the purpose of relationships at work is to enhance the success of the enterprise* – is, for most people, easy to understand and to even agree with. "I get it", people say, and then ask, "But what do I do with it? If this is as true as it logically seems, then how do I proceed?" *What does it even mean to anyone on a practical, day-to-day basis, to know that the purpose of your relationships at work is to forward the success of the company?*

Until you know the purpose of anything that you do, you don't really have the opportunity to knowingly fulfill that purpose. You can make up anything in the absence of knowing. The most common response to the question "What is the purpose of your relationships at work?" is a blank look, because it doesn't even register as a sensible question.

## What do you do with that?

There is a distinct advantage in asking the question of one's self. Because when you see the answer, then your ability to fulfill on that purpose becomes way more likely. When you see it, it makes sense, and when it makes sense, you can act on it. The question we asked ourselves was: "Well, what do we do with that?"

The answer, finally, became you do what you're here to do. You engage with each person in a way that supports their ability to be successful at their job. And they in turn, help others be more successful at their jobs. And in that way, you and everyone else are fulfilling your purpose. Every encounter with a fellow employee becomes an opportunity to help the company be more successful.

40

*Meet y Joe*

There is nothing else. Your relationships at work are importa
and they're important because if everybody is successful at their
jobs then the organization is going to be successful.

*Signed Mary PM*

### So what do you talk about?

In case it isn't already obvious, we introduced the concept
of the execution cycle, and certainly, one thing you do when
you talk to others at work is to get an execution cycle started
and moving forward. Any request is an invitation to start a
cycle. Also, you can make offers to others. In our language, an
offer accepted can be construed as a request, and a request is an
invitation for an acceptance (a promise) or a refusal to accept.
You can also negotiate; e.g., "I can't get that report to you by
Friday. However, would Monday afternoon work for you?"
Learning to communicate more effectively with others takes
practice. And in the beginning of practice, of all practice, there
is some clumsiness. The execution cycle ought to be a critical
part of your interactions with others, and you want these pointed
interactions to further your relationships, not be something that
gets in the way.

It is important to remember that you're not the execution
police. You are a co-worker who is invested in the success of
everybody around you. There are people to whom you report.
If you are a manager or an executive there are people that report
to you. You are their partner, whether they are your manager or
you are theirs. You both want the same thing: *their success and
yours along with the success of the company.* One very successful
senior executive in a large company told us he practices "gentle
accountability" (we promote that practice). You never need to be
angry or upset in moving execution cycles along. You can always

be civil. Sometimes this may not be easy, like when someone who reports to you is continually failing at doing what he said he was going to do and you have to explain to him that his job is at stake. It might not be easy, but you need to do what you need to do.

Not all conversations at work are going to be requests and promises. You might have conversations on the progress of a project, or an issue to discuss, or to collaborate on creating a new marketing campaign, and so on. Here's the point: you want all of these types of conversations conducted in a way that is helping to further the success of the company. In addition, there is a need to be civil to each other, to be respectful of one another, to show each other that you're interested in them, and so on.

You may want to have these types of conversations too: How are you doing? How can I help you? Let me tell you how you can help me. How do you think I could be better at what I do? May I offer some suggestions to you? How could we work together better? How are you doing with your goals? What is getting in your way? What is the secret to your success?

You get the idea.

## What else do you need to do?

You *do need* to be clear about your job responsibilities and goals, and to have those around you be clear about theirs. You *do need* you and your manager to be on the same page about what the organization expects of you, as you need to have that same clarity with any employees that report to you. You *do need* to have everybody in your organization to have clear reminders about what the vision, mission, core behaviors and key initiatives are, so everyone maximizes that clear line of sight to what's important to the organization. You *do need* to have ī meetings to discuss progress with your manager and also with your employees so that everybody's chances of being successful are maximized. You *do need* to have some means of discovering what needs to be discussed in order to remove blocks to success.

You're going to need an execution management system to help you and we recommend you find one and use it. It will help you clarify your job responsibilities and your goals and keep track of your progress so that others can help you. We also recommend performance agreements (between an employee and their manager) that are flexible so that you can stay clear and aligned with your manager and/or your employee about what everybody is doing. And we recommend progress meetings between employees and their managers so that you can build the relationship with your manager and your employee that will maximize results for all. A system enables all that. We'll discuss more about execution management systems, performance agreements, and progress meetings in a later chapter.

**There is more**

If the relationship with each other matters, then the quality of each relationship matters. Trust matters, and trust emerges from the core commitment to being trustworthy – primarily to do what you said you were going to do when you said you were going to do it, to minimize but keep confidentialities, and to tell the truth as you know it. Caring counts. Being of service to others counts. Respect counts.

Relationships require attention. If you're paying attention, you'll know when there appears to be some break in the relationship. For the most part, people step over these breaks in relationships at work. Make it your business to seek resolution. This is part of the effort to develop truly good relationships. If relationships matter, you need to treat them like they matter. If you need to, ask questions like this: "Are you having some problem with me?"; "Are you angry at me for something?"; "Have I said or done something that offended you?"; "How are you and I doing as team members?"; "I'm sensing some tension in our relationship, is something going on?" There are a myriad of possibilities. Ask these questions as a concerned partner, not as an accuser. There's a saying, "You can never over-communicate", and it's probably true. If you have a problem, ask if they're willing to discuss something with you, and tell them how you are feeling about what happened. Make sure it is not an indictment, nor an accusation. "It seemed to me you were angry at me, and I felt hurt by that" is a safe model for describing your experience. "You got angry at me and it pisses me off" is not a good or safe model for describing your experience.

**The Time It Takes**

Very few people at work these days have a lot of spare time. Often when we have this conversation with clients for the first time, they say, "Yeah but..." and the "but" refers to the fact that they don't have the time. If you don't have the time to tend to your relationships at work, you don't have enough time to do your job and something needs to change.

We believe the activity of any management position is best spent working with what we call the "critical relationships" with whom you work. Generally, the critical relationships you have are your direct reports, whoever you report to, and sometimes your peers or some of your peers. There could be others, depending on the type of work you do. In other words, if you are in a management position, you have an investment in the person you report to and you have an investment in the people who report to you. If these people are successful, you're going to be successful, and if you're going to be successful, they are also going to be successful. This is why we say you should consider your critical people your partners.

So our answer to people in management who say they don't have the time is "What else do you have to do that's more important?" Your job as a manager is to have the people around you be successful.

For most managers, we recommend having a regular time every week that you spend with your direct reports, not just to get updated about what they're doing but to connect with them, see how they're doing, find out how you could help them, share with them any concerns you have, and talk to them about anything that you feel is unspoken between you. In other words, use these available opportunities to build your working relationships.

What "normally" happens at work is we ignore the breakdowns in our relationships. We step over them. But think about this: if someone is angry at you for something you said or did, and they don't communicate it with you with an intention to let it go, then what happens? They put it aside in their mind and the next time they don't like something you say or do, they add that to what now is becoming a pile of resentment and before long they have a negative opinion about you that's getting worse. If you now link that with the fact that you are partners in each other's success, can you see what the problem is? Do you see how

45

your partnership is eroding? Do you really believe people want you to be successful who have resentment or negative judgments or hurt feelings about you?

And what about you? Do you really want people, whom you have built a case against in your mind, to succeed? Now, be truthful. The answer for most of us would be "not really". Relationships at work matter and it takes work for them to matter.

Once again, we're going over something in a relatively short span of written information that deserves its own book.

## Summary

The purpose of relationships at work is to enhance the success of the enterprise. This means what you're doing with each other and what you're talking about are the important aspects of their work and your work, and how each is progressing. Relationships at work matter and the quality of your relationships at work matter. This takes some doing, some attention, some work, and some learning.

If relationships matter – and they do – then the quality matters. This means you need to pay attention to them. You need to dedicate time for them. You need to be vigilant with your own thoughts and learn the skills of building mutually empowering working relationships. What else do you have to do that's more important?

This is the world of the future. It is the fulfillment of what we organizationally and individually should envision.

# NOTES

_____

_____

_____

_____

_____

_____

_____

_____

_____

_____

_____

_____

_____

_____

_____

_____

_____

_____

_____

_____

_____

_____

_____

# NOTES

# NOTES

# ❧ *Chapter 5* ❧

# Commitment:
# the Secret Sauce

*"You always have two choices: your commitment versus your fear."*

Sammy Davis Jr.

*"This may sound too simple, but is great in consequence. Until one is committed, there is hesitancy, the chance to draw back, always ineffectiveness. Concerning all acts of initiative (and creation), there is one elementary truth the ignorance of which kills countless ideas and splendid plans: that the moment one definitely commits oneself, then providence moves too. A whole stream of events issues from the decision, raising in one's favor all manner of unforeseen incidents, meetings and material assistance, which no man could have dreamt would have come his way. I learned a deep respect for one of Goethe's couplets:*

*Whatever you can do or dream you can, begin it. Boldness has genius, power and magic in it!"*

William H. Murray, Scottish conqueror of Mt. Everest

Where there is no commitment, there is no accomplishment beyond "whatever". We can try to do better; we can struggle; we can be well-intended. And we might incrementally improve, and that's not a bad thing. But will we accomplish anything out of the ordinary? Will we go beyond what can be expected? Will we achieve extraordinary results? Will we invent anything of importance? Will we master anything?

Without commitment, we would not have a light bulb, or an airplane. We would not have gone to the moon (which means, we're told, we would not have invented the GPS). We would not have any of the technological advances we have made over the last hundred years or so. Thomas Edison is said to have failed 10,000 times in the process of inventing the light bulb. What kept him going, if not commitment? He said he was going to do it, and he did. What kept the Wright brothers persisting after so many failures? Without commitment, what world-changing movement would have occurred? And on a smaller scale, how many people would have completed a marathon? How would Rocky Balboa have won the championship? How would Sylvester Stallone ever have made the first "Rocky" movie?

Imagine a world without commitment. If you really do that, really imagine it, you'll know what we're talking about. The "secret sauce" is no secret anymore.

Think of a commitment as a declaration that you're going to do something or accomplish something that generally takes some time and often involves other people. Note that we used the word *declaration*; the dictionary and common usage say agreement. A declaration is another one of those *performative* speech acts – when you declare something you're stating that this will be so, and the act of declaring is the performance of that act.

52

A commitment then, as a declaration, is you saying some future event will happen because you have committed yourself to it.

## Commitments vs. Promises

We distinguish a difference between a commitment and a promise, and we do it for the reason that it's useful in the context of mastering execution.

As already stated, a commitment is a declaration, but it must be one you have the authority or the right to make. When you're accountable for something, you have the right to commit, and arguably an expectation to do so. On the other hand, declaring the world will end by a certain date is not in most of our job descriptions (and we have a lot of evidence that those are really predictions, not declarations, and they are, so far, all meaningless – thankfully).

If you're fifty years old, not in good physical shape, and 5'6" in height, you probably don't have the right to declare that you're going to be a professional basketball player in the NBA. You can say whatever you want, but you saying it, doesn't make it so. To actually commit yourself to it may make for an interesting adventure, and it may lead to being in better physical shape, or maybe someone will make a video of your story that will go viral, but it isn't going to lead to your being drafted by the New York Knicks.

We have worked with a lot of people over the years and have been in conversations with them about what is or what isn't possible. We like to say that nothing is impossible, but, on the other hand, there's a difference between attempting to accomplish something that is a stretch for you and something that is far-fetched and way out of reach. There's an art to setting stretch goals that only comes with experience. The experience very often goes like this: you set your initiatives for this year, and find that you set them too ambitiously; the next year you swing the other way by setting them too modestly; and so on. Sooner or later, you get good at it. If you're aware of this tendency, you'll become artful at it much sooner.

Perhaps more to the point, *if you don't say it and commit yourself to it,* the likelihood you're going to accomplish it is very slim. If you don't know the place for commitments in your journey to the mastery of execution, you're going to have a difficult journey and it's not going to end up where you want it to.

It's critical to know this – if you commit to something, it must imply you mean it. You know it's not going to be easy, but you're ready to do whatever you have to do (note that every time we express this we mean "so whatever you have to do within the limits of legal, moral, ethical, and other such boundaries"). If you really mean it, and you have the authority and the will to make it happen, you need to manage yourself from there in order to have it come about. You're saying you will do this, that you will do whatever you have to do, that you will overcome all of the barriers and that you will stick with it in order to have it be accomplished.

Obviously, sometimes you'll make commitments and really mean it, but fail. If you succeed at all of your commitments, you're probably not setting the bar high enough. To accomplish mastery of execution at a high level, you want to get yourself to a place where most of the times when you commit to something, you achieve it.

We have already established that a promise is made in order to fulfill on something that you've been asked to do or that you've offered to do. It is relatively basic in nature and will often not involve other people. For example, you can meet with your manager in his office tomorrow morning at 9:00 AM. You can promise that, but it doesn't necessarily mean something won't happen along the way that will throw you off. You'll still do what you can to make it happen, but if some emergency comes up and you can't make it, you'll call and let your manager know and then re-schedule if possible. You have an intention to keep your promises, but as we've said before, *nobody keeps all of their promises.* The point here is if you just can't keep a promise, apologize and let the other person know that it was unavoidable. You want them to know that you take your word seriously and that you can be counted on in the future.

A commitment is more complex. It's a response to a larger request, but it's a request that a simple promise won't cover. For example, let's say it's an initiative or a project or a result that you can't really promise because you don't know for sure that you can do it. However, you're declaring that you'll do whatever it takes to succeed at it. A corporation often makes forecasts for the year to its shareholders and board, but these are generally considered predictions, not commitments. Often, as the year progresses, the CEO will make adjustments to these forecasts, sometimes quarterly. What we would want to know, if we were on their board, is not what they are predicting they are going to do, but what they are going to do. There is no commitment in a prediction. The weather people make predictions every day and perhaps at some point if their predictions continue to be wrong, they'll lose their credibility. However, their job is not to commit to what they say the weather will be tomorrow. In the organizational d, predictions may be useful, but commitments have much more meaning and produce more meaningful results.

Here's more on the difference between commitments and promises:

- A promise is saying you'll do something you can do.

- A commitment, you have less control over. It generally involves others. It is complex and it should be a stretch. You're saying you'll do it, but you don't necessarily know if you can or can't. The assumption is you can, even if you don't know how. If you already know how to do a "stretch target" commitment, it's probably not stretch enough.

- By making a commitment, you're willing to go beyond what we usually call "doing my best". "Doing my best" easily becomes an excuse. It falls into the category of a saying by author Richard Bach: "Argue for your limitations and sure enough they're yours." Doing your best can become – and often does become – I do what my limitations allow. A commitment often requires going beyond your limitations and that is one of the reasons why it is so powerful.

- If you can see how "I will do my best" differs from "I am committed to achieving this" you understand commitment and the power of it. Saying you will "do your best" or "I'll do what I can" can be a cop-out. You don't know what you can do and you don't know what your best is. In a way, when you say this, you're saying "I will do what I believe is all I can do", but what if your belief is a mistaken one? Haven't you ever had a belief that turned out to be wrong? Can you see that what you believe you can do or what you can't do defines what your limits are? Every time you say you'll "do your best" you are declaring that you have limits. And haven't you ever gone beyond your limits? The power of commitment is that you place yourself in a situation where, most likely, you'll need to go beyond what you think of as your limits.

- A commitment is like a tunnel that you put yourself into in order to go beyond what you might do if you weren't in that tunnel. It ought to be considered a tunnel of no return. Of course this isn't true, there's always a way out, but if you close those escapes in your thinking you'll be able to go beyond what you think you can.

- If you keep your promises, what could be said about you is that you're someone who keeps their word. This is a great thing to be known for. It's also a beginning practice of execution mastery.

- If you fulfill your commitments, it can be said that you deliver. There is no one more valuable to themselves or to an organization than someone who commits as a matter of course and delivers on their commitments. If you are an executive or a manager, this comprises your dream staff – people who can be counted on to deliver.

- No one can force you to commit. A commitment (in the sense we're using the word) is a choice, no matter how much or how little pressure is put on you. If you are pressured and you just say you're committed, the odds are you'll not be successful because you're not really committed, you're just being compliant. It takes some degree of boldness to choose to be committed. If you're not really committed, what good is it? You can pretend to be committed, but if you aren't producing the expected results, it's not going to get you very far.

- Some people insist that promises are commitments – a commitment to deliver on your promise. They make a good argument for it, and it's technically right. We've found, though, that distinguishing promises from commitments is more useful than calling a promise a commitment. We're more interested in the language of greatness than we are in being technically right.

- Commitments, being complex and often involving other people, usually require more elaborate plans. You commit to a result, you plan for its accomplishment, and then you work your plan. The steps to the plan must be considered promises. For example, you've made a commitment to a goal of having revenues of one hundred million dollars this year. You have a plan, and you and your team understand the plan consists of a number of promises that you have made together, and you follow the plan and adjust the plan as needed. Assume you and your team have the experience to conceive a good plan and you have the ability to do what the plan requires. The odds that you'll be successful go way up, if each of you is genuinely committed. Wouldn't you agree? Can you see where you can, over time, get to a place where it's very likely you'll achieve your commitments?

- If you consider your key organizational initiatives to be commitments, and the individual responsibilities and goals related to those initiatives as commitments, imagine the power and the possibilities. If you add to the mix that you are committed to mastering execution, and to renewing your commitment year after

year, what could your organization achieve in
come? Or, better yet, what couldn't your orgaᵢ
achieve?

Don't just skip over what we've just asked. No kidding, think
about it! This is what this book is all about. What couldn't be
achieved?

**Summary**

A commitment is a declaration to accomplish something
within a period of time that stretches capability. You might think
of it as a muscle that you're developing – the ability to say you're
going to tackle an objective that is difficult and be successful at it
no matter what. It means you become someone who can deliver.
It is distinguished from a promise in that a promise is something
you know you can do and a commitment is something that you
don't know from past experiences that you can achieve, but by
the act of committing to it, the likelihood that you'll be successful
excels. Without commitment, there is very little hope of anything
extraordinary, of anything beyond what you've always done.
Without commitment, the journey to mastery of execution is
going to be long and arduous and not very satisfying.

Taking the journey to the mastery of execution is
extraordinary, and so are the results that ensue.

# NOTES

## NOTES

_____

_____

_____

_____

_____

_____

_____

_____

_____

_____

_____

_____

_____

_____

_____

_____

_____

_____

_____

_____

_____

_____

_____

# *Chapter 6*

# Managing Execution

*"Leading for execution is not about micromanaging, or being 'hands-on', or disempowering people. Rather, it's about active involvement – doing the things leaders should be doing in the first place."*

Bossidy and Charan,
*Execution: The Discipline of Getting Things Done*

No matter what title you have and regardless of what you do in your vocation, if you're going to master execution in your organization you have to manage execution. If you don't manage it, you're not going to optimize your ability to execute, and over time you're not going to soar above mediocrity. *Managing execution is not just a good idea; it is required!*

Keep in mind that before you discovered execution, there was nothing there to manage. The discovery of execution rescues it from being non-existent, except as a concept. Since execution was always there – like air – it's always needed to be managed, but it was always managed randomly and even blindly. Ironically, before we actually discovered execution ourselves, when we would talk to executives about managing execution, their first reaction was always to say, "We already do that". When we asked them what they were doing to manage execution, they would say they have a dashboard or they have Excel spreadsheets or they have performance reviews, and so on. We started addressing the issue early on with executives by asking them, "Do you have a system that you use to manage execution?" One of the CEOs we asked this question to remained silent for a moment, and then he started laughing. He said, "I have a system, but it's a rabble!" We laughed with him. But as soon as we got back to the office we looked up the word rabble to find out what it really meant. A rabble is, according to the dictionary, "*a disorganized or confused collection of things*".

Most senior executives believe they have systems in place to manage execution. The problem is this: it's not really a system. It's a bunch of, at best, loosely related processes for accomplishing different apparent aspects of execution. Whenever we got into the details with executives about what they did to manage execution they usually enumerated on a number of the different things they do. The following is a typical dialogue we've had:

"Do those things work for you?"

They most often would take each activity they had mentioned and would give it an off-the-cuff score: "This one works pretty well. This one…I don't know. This one is a necessity", and so on.

When they were done, we would ask; "So, would you call this, taken all together, a system?"

"Uh…no, I guess not."

"Would you say your company has a core competence in managing execution or in execution itself?"

They usually answered "No" and it was often accompanied by a laugh.

We don't mean to make fun of what you're doing now in your organization, nor would we diminish the value of all of the things organizations do to track and manage performance. It's just that without a system, you're not ever going to master execution. It would be like trying to drive a car without a drivetrain (which, according to Wikipedia, is the group of components that deliver power to the driving wheels).

We strongly recommend using what's called an *execution management system*, which we will go into shortly. A formal execution management system is not necessarily required, although at some point in time, it just makes sense to utilize one. If you don't have some system, though, you're going to have just what you have now – a bunch of disjointed activities that don't really improve your ability to execute.

When we first started using an execution management system with our clients, we found they were seeing good results right away. We soon discovered that what we used to do with clients in helping them with execution could now be done better, in less time, and for less money by using a system. And the likelihood they would continue to get better in execution and execution management was much higher. In other words, those using an execution management system sustained their usage of it over time.

But after a few years we realized we had slipped into a mindset of *the tool being more important than the purpose of the tool,* and our clients were doing the same. We realized the context wasn't big enough. The context needed to be the mastery of execution, not the utility of the execution management system. Without the context – and without the commitment – the tool was becoming "just another thing to do", and its usefulness and power was starting to ebb. An execution management system is an enabler and a very powerful accelerator of this process, but it should never be confused with the purpose for its existence. A hammer exists so you can bang in the nail – it's not about the hammer. *What an execution management system is all about is helping you fulfill on your commitment to the mastery of execution.*

One client in particular was experiencing a problem that actually inspired our awakening to the need for this context shift. A new C-suite hire at our client's manufacturing company was very resistant to using their execution management system. And because of the importance of his position there, it constituted a major breach in the system. "Help me", the CEO pleaded. We found ourselves saying the following to him, which proved to be our approach with every client who had a similar issue and we offer it to you:

*What execution mgt system do you recommend?* (handwritten)

"*You do not need to require that anyone on your team uses the system. However, you do need to require that everyone that reports to you is clear about the organizational vision, the mission, the core behavioral expectations, and what the key focuses need to be this year. You also do need to have them draft an agreement about what they will focus on and accomplish this year, which will begin a discussion that will result in its being approved by you. This agreement will be the central topic of discussion in a monthly progress meeting with you, so that together you can work toward their success.*

"*In addition, you do need to require that each of your direct reports needs to get the same from each of their direct reports, and so on until every level of management is doing the same thing. Lastly, the success of the entire pyramid of employees under each manager is the responsibility of that manager.*

"*Now, I don't care much about the format of how you do that, as long as it's easy enough for me to use with you and track. It seems to me that since I do require this, it makes sense for you to learn the system we already have in place, but I'll leave that up to you. I don't care as much about the system as I do care about the organization's success and your success, and about our getting better and better in our ability to execute.*"

The above describes what it means to us to manage execution.

## What Matters in Managing Execution

The following is a list of what to keep in mind when managing execution. It is not meant to be an exhaustive list, nor is it in any particular order of importance. All of them are important:

## Relationships matter

We wrote about this in chapter 4. Relationships do matter. Tend to them. Consider them when managing execution. Do not become the execution police. Become instead an execution leader, learner, and partner to others around you.

## Leadership matters

There are a lot of definitions on leadership. This is one of our favorite definitions on leadership that comes from Jim Hunter, author of *The World's Most Powerful Leadership Principle: How to Become a Servant Leader*:

> "Leadership is influencing people to willingly, even enthusiastically, contribute their hearts, minds, creativity, excellence, and other resources toward mutually beneficial goals. Leadership is influencing people to commit to the vision and mission. Leadership is influencing people to become the best they are capable of becoming."

## The vision and mission matter

*what is ans?*

Vision and mission serve as your North Star. They give you direction and a common purpose for everyone in your organization. No common compelling future equals nothing extraordinary is going to happen.

68

## Focus matters

In terms of momentum in execution, focus is everything. In a sense, managing execution means managing focus. If people stay focused on the right things, you are managing execution and you're going to see the results you want. What could be simpler than that?

*too many formulate this.*

## Developing people matters

If you are a leader or a manager or both in your organization and you've been doing it for a few years, you know that the future of the company depends on the development of the people that work there. This means not just the "high potentials", but everybody. If you're generating an organization in which people are committed to mastery of execution, think about what you're doing. You're developing people to deliver and having them develop others who deliver. What more could you want?

## The right level of involvement matters

As a manager or a leader, there is a right level of involvement with the people who report to you that is essential. Without this right level of involvement they will not be optimally successful nor continue to develop. However, if you go beyond that right level you could squelch their blossoming. Not only do you have to find this level for yourself, you also have to find the right level for each individual that you manage.

**The execution management system matters**

An execution management system makes it easier to stay on track and do all of the things you need to do to manage the execution in your organization. It also makes it easier to manage your own individual work life. Once you've used an execution management system for a while, you can't imagine working without it.

Execution management systems are relatively new and there aren't that many in existence yet. Most of the ones we're familiar with are good in theory but are difficult to implement and almost impossible to sustain. We knew there had to be a system out there that was easy enough to use; affordable for our clients; compatible with our beliefs on execution, leadership and alignment; and was sustainable. We found that system. It's called KeyneLink. We have been using it with our clients ever since. It was developed by Keyne Insight (www.keyneinsight.com) and we think enough of it to mention it here. We work with our clients to help them understand how to use the system and how to implement it throughout their organizations. It soon becomes an indispensable aid to their organizational and individual journeys to the mastery of execution.

We've been serving as senior advisors to Wayne Nelsen, the co-founder of KeyneLink and Keyne Insight, and in turn, he's been serving as a senior advisor to us. We've had hundreds of hours of conversations between the three of us and a lot of what we're writing about in this book has been influenced by those discussions. We've also been influenced by the language and concepts that were developed by Keyne Insight. Prime examples are *performance agreements, progress meetings, core behaviors and primary job responsibilities.* Our own learning curve – relative to

execution and execution mastery – has accelerated tremen̲u̲
and it increases exponentially the more we use KeyneLink as an
adjunct to the journey to mastery of execution with our clients.

Briefly, KeyneLink helps you organize around execution.
It is a system for managing execution which includes cloud-
based software as a focusing mechanism. The system basically
posits that if you are grounded in, and have easy access to, your
organization's foundation data (vision, mission, core behaviors,
and initiatives), and if you have performance agreements with
each of key people in your organization, and if you have it all
organized and lined up so you can track and support progress
regularly as you go along, then that constitutes the bare bones of
managing execution. If done well, you'll maximize your success,
the development of your people and your learning to get better
and better at execution – not just for a little while, but year after
year.

There are other execution management systems; in fact, they're
a rapidly growing phenomenon. Our strong recommendation
for having the surest pathway to execution mastery is that you
find a consultant/coach who can help you and ask them for their
advice on a system. Then jump on that train.

An execution management system will serve as your
guardrails for staying the course in your journey. It will not only
give you the focus you need but it will enable your commitment to
accelerating your learning and capability as you proceed forward.
Just remember, don't let the execution management system be
more important than the purpose of mastering execution.

**Who is accountable for execution in your company?**

The answer, of course, is everybody. But taking the case that single-point accountability works, someone needs the overall accountability. Typically, that's the CEO or the president or the owner. We also know that there are people in positions of leadership that are accountable for separate functions or divisions. For example, the CFO is responsible for the financial management, the CIO is responsible for the technology, the COO is responsible for operations, and so on. But when it comes to execution, most organizations leave that responsibility to their employees, which means that no one has assumed the overall responsibility and accountability for execution.

*We are making a case for having a Chief Execution Officer, or CXO.*

The CXO's job is to make sure that the organization is fulfilling its commitments to its initiatives; that in general everybody is learning to get better and better at execution; that the enterprise is organized to maximize effectiveness; that everyone who is in a management position is utilizing best practices in producing results; that the execution management system is being used to maximize its effectiveness in managing progress and learning; and in general is cultivating a culture of accelerating capability.

*If a CXO is successful, then the company is going to be phenomenally successful.*

We assert that this notion of a CXO is a critical missing piece of the puzzle in the business world. We discovered this missing piece and have recently started introducing it to our clients. At this time, it would be very difficult to find someone who could fill this seat at the C-suite table. Our company, The Kierson Tomlinson Group, as consultants and coaches, take the position of interim CXO and, as we're going along, we're training someone in our client organizations to be the CXO. In companies too small to add another C-level position on the payroll, we recommend either the CEO or the COO add CXO to their titles – e.g., John Smith, Chief Executive Officer and Chief Execution Officer.

## Summary

To repeat an early line in this chapter, "Managing execution is not just a good idea; it is required." It's required because if you don't have a system to manage execution, what you have is a plethora of different tools and practices that are mostly unrelated to each other, and together do not constitute a system. A system says the Merriam-Webster dictionary, is a group of related parts that move or work together. In organizational parlance, if the management of execution coordinates it to move and work together toward specific ends, the likelihood you're going to accomplish what you set out to accomplish goes way up. Without a system you're just playing Russian roulette with the results.

As we stated in the first chapter, execution as a capability, is real. It needs attention and it needs management and it needs oversight. The position of a Chief Execution Officer (CXO) is a critical but until now overlooked addition to the executive body of any organization, whether it is a separate position or an added responsibility to an existing senior leader.

# NOTES

_____

_____

_____

_____

_____

_____

_____

_____

_____

_____

_____

_____

_____

_____

_____

_____

_____

_____

_____

_____

_____

_____

_____

_____

# NOTES

# ᘒ *Chapter 7* ᘒ

# The Journey to
# Mastery of Execution

*"True mastery, it turns out, is not found in accumulating each and every tool under the sun. True mastery is learning that there are really only a handful of tools, and it is the proper application with correct timing and setting that makes them so useful."*

Chris Matakas,
*My Mastery: Continued Education Through Jiu Jitsu*

By now, you're beginning to discover execution or maybe you have already discovered it. Briefly, it takes *a blinding flash of the ever-present* – the realization that execution exists. There's a language that enables it, in particular the essential element of the execution cycle. It requires a continued focus and management, including overcoming fear and resistance associated with it. It requires the acknowledgment of the importance of relationships and the willingness to give at least critical relationships the attention they demand.

Finally, the journey to mastery of execution, at some point takes commitment. We maintain that rarely, if ever, does one take on the journey to mastery of anything – a martial art, the playing of a musical instrument, a sport, dancing, painting, writing, and so on – without first learning the basics and becoming more familiar with what it entails. If you went to a dojo, never having begun any practice, and stated that you wanted to be a black belt, the sensei might laugh. He would probably tell you to practice with them for a year and then see if you still wanted to aspire to be a master. And if you do, you can then take on the commitment. It is foolish to make a commitment to something you know so little about.

We said earlier that nothing extraordinary was ever accomplished without commitment. Without a doubt, the mastery of execution is extraordinary and takes commitment. Committing is an individual act and you can commit as an individual. For an organization to take on the mastery of execution, it takes the commitment of a minimum of one person who is the leader with the willingness to garner the commitment of a team of leaders, who in turn will amass a number of others to cause a tipping point. This not only takes willingness, but also vision, time, skill, endurance, and practice.

If that seems like a daunting task, consider these two differences between mastering execution and mastering most of those other endeavors we mentioned:

1. To learn to play the violin, for instance, you're going to need to take lessons and practice. All of which are in addition to how you make your living; or, if you're student, in addition to your going to school. To learn dancing requires time in the studio and practice at home. Aikido takes time in the dojo and exercise at home. However, execution practice happens while you're working. It doesn't require much else – what we like to call "no time" because it doesn't require hardly any extra time.

2. While you're learning on the job, from the very beginning, you're improving your ability to execute as well as impacting others around you to improve their execution skills as well. You are not just learning; you're getting better at execution as you go along, individually and as an organization. Even if you only get a little better at execution in the first year, you're going to see substantial gains in the results at work. And that will continue to accelerate, year after year.

## What is mastery, anyway?

If you're beginning to think execution mastery is for you and your organization, it would be useful to at least be introduced to the notion of mastery so that you can get a taste of what that journey will entail.

One learns mastery by aspiring for it and practicing it. There is a terrific book on mastery that we recommend to our clients. It's called *Mastery: The Keys to Success and Long-Term Fulfillment*, written by the late George Leonard. Leonard had been an educator and then, relatively late in his life, had taken up the study and practice of the Japanese martial art known as Aikido, and was considered a master of it. If you're considering taking up the mastery of anything, we strongly recommend this small book to you. We quote it often, as we will here in this chapter. It's a small book and can be read in a couple of hours, although it's probably worth reading more slowly.

> *"What is mastery? At the heart of it, mastery is practice. Mastery is staying on the path."*

That's what Leonard says mastery is. It's a combination of practice and staying on the path. To master something involves the answer to the question, "How do you get to Carnegie Hall?" – practice, practice, practice. To practice diligently over time is to confront drudgery, frustration, the eschewing of comfortability, and, ultimately, resistance. It's not an easy journey, but it's well worth it, not just because you end up being really, really good at something, but also because the practice itself becomes a joy. As Leonard says:

> *"The real juice of life, whether it be sweet or bitter, is to be found not nearly so much in the products of our efforts as in the process of living itself, in how it feels to be alive."*

What does mastery of execution look like in an organization? Truly, we don't exactly know, because it's a journey without end. We can tell you how we would define it, though, at least as a first level of mastery. The organization that reflects the mastery of execution is one in which:

1. Stretch targets are set every year; and, year after year, the organization achieves those targets more often than not (approximately 75% - 80%). We always say "more often than not" for two reasons: (1) if you always hit your targets, you're not setting them high enough, and (2) in the world of organization, unpredictable things happen. For example there are market changes, there are natural disasters, there's new technology that can change everything, there's new competition, etc. Part of mastering execution is learning to meet the challenges, but sometimes you just won't be able to do so (that's why they call them *challenges*).

2. It's a great place to work, not because it's easy, but because it provides an environment of challenge, growth, opportunity, meaning, and worth of both the individual and of the organization itself. It also has a culture of what one of our client's calls "gentle accountability." In other words, employees know how to be accountable and help others be accountable without beating them up.

One of our favorite quotes is from John F. Kennedy, then president of the United States in 1962. It's from a speech that he made to declare the country's *commitment* to going to the moon by the end of the decade (you can find and hear this speech on YouTube). After making this commitment, as the story goes, many people around President Kennedy told him it couldn't be done. Scientists were among them: they said, "We don't have the fuel to do this." And Kennedy responded with, "Then invent it!" Kennedy did not live to see it, but he set things in motion, and before the end of the decade, the U.S. landed on the moon and the astronauts returned safely back to Earth.

Here's the quote:

> *"We choose to go to the moon in this decade and to do these other things not because they are easy, but because they are hard, because that goal will serve to organize and measure the best of our energies and skills, because that challenge is one that we are willing to accept, one we are unwilling to postpone, and one which we intend to win."*

It's in this spirit that the commitment to mastery of execution can be made. The above is our most basic idea of what an organization that has achieved a level of mastery is like. Wouldn't you want to work for a company that chooses to "go to the moon"? It's not meant to be a substitute for what your vision is, or will be. We're not telling you what you should aspire to; we are inviting you to aspire to something beyond your current reach, to "invent the fuel", and to inspire others along the way. This is called leadership.

We worked with a client that, one year, had on the cover of their annual report, "We Said...", and then on the next page, "We Did". They showed the goals they had said they were going to accomplish on their annual report the year before and then they showed their results, which matched or exceeded their intentions. They said they were going to do this and they did it. To us, this is inspiring. It's so much easier to say, "Well, I know I said I was going to accomplish those things, but, well, I ran into this situation and that situation and..." As a colleague of ours likes to say;

> *"Execution does not equal poor performance plus good excuses."*

George Leonard again:

*"We fail to realize that mastery is not about perfection. It's about a process, a journey. The master is the one who stays on the path day after day, year after year. The master is the one who is willing to try, and fail, and try again, for as long as he lives."*

## The Journey Itself

As everybody knows, every journey starts with the first step, and the first step to the journey to mastery of execution is to make the commitment to it. This means you (1) start learning and practicing it, (2) reach a point in which you're ready to be committed to it, (3) commit to it, and (4) resume from where you are now on the journey but with a different level of intentional investment from hereon in. We might add (5) stick to it.

We'll talk more about this later in the book, but we strongly recommend that you hire a consultant or a coach who knows enough about execution to help you get on a path to learn the right practices to get you going. One of those practices will need to be committing to an execution management system. Without it, it's likely you won't get very far with your overall attempt to learn to be better at execution. That's because you'll get distracted and frustrated and you'll start justifying to yourself and to your organization that either it's not working or that it's not worth the effort. What isn't worth the effort is a half-baked testing of the waters only to re-discover the futility of working without at least the minimal commitment of utilizing a coach, a system, and a plan for staying the course.

It's our experience that for an organization to get to the point at which they are ready to commit to the journey to mastery of execution takes anywhere from a half a year to a year. Even if you never make the commitment to the full journey, you'll have gained enormously in terms of your individual learning and improved results in your work. You really have nothing to lose. You'll see a return on your investment many times over – not just for this first year, but for year-after-year as long as you continue to practice what you've learned.

If you do commit, know that it takes a few years to begin to approach mastery. However, with the right program you'll benefit more and more each and every year. The most important practice you can take on for mastery of execution is the practice of continuing to have an orientation to learning, no matter how good you get. You'll discover if you do this whole-heartedly, you'll never get tired of the journey because it energizes you. As George Leonard says; *"The master is the one who stays on the path day after day, year after year…as long as he lives."*

We're not saying you have to do this as long as you live; rather, just as long as you're working. Execution mastery is not the ticket to heaven. However, it is a ticket to success. The real answer to "How long does it take to get there?" is you'll never get "there", although you'll reach a point in time where you are masterful. You'll never get there because you're always learning and you'll continue to get better and better for as long as you want to. Anybody who is great at anything, whether it's a sport or an art or even execution will tell you that he or she still strives to learn and improve, as long as they're still active.

We can't overstate the importance of having a learning attitude. If you're always learning, you can't fail. Thomas Edison

said, *"I haven't failed. I've just found 10,000 ways that won't work."*
You will never reach perfection in execution and we should be grateful for that. However, what you can do is you can lead the pack of companies that are in your industry. You can achieve great heights. You can contribute enormously to the world.

## Summary

The journey to mastery of execution takes commitment, but unlike most other mastery endeavors, you'll get better and better at it from the very beginning. You'll profit in your work and your practice takes place as you work. It could even be said that your work is your practice. Mastery is practice. The path is one of beginning, committing and doing the things that are required – keep practicing, find a qualified consultant/coach, adopt an execution management system, and keep on learning. *We promise it's a journey you'll never regret.*

# NOTES

# NOTES

_____

_____

_____

_____

_____

_____

_____

_____

_____

_____

_____

_____

_____

_____

_____

_____

_____

_____

_____

_____

_____

_____

_____

# Chapter 8

# The Resistance to Getting Better at Execution

*"Only three things happen naturally in organizations; one is friction, two is confusion and three is underperformance. Everything else requires leadership."*

Peter Drucker

We first became acutely aware of the resistance to getting better at execution at an executive team workshop we conducted in the early 2000s. We were working with a company that was not only fourth quartile in their industry; they were fourth quartile of the fourth quartile, way down at the bottom of the list of companies in terms of their significant and competitive results. The current team had inherited years and years of worsening capabilities and had a really poor culture of *no accountability*. Everybody in attendance knew there was a lot that needed to be changed.

We spent a fair amount of time on accountability, addressing the practices for this team of leaders in order to break their habitual way of doing things. We discussed what execution is and its importance. We explained and even practiced the execution cycle. We talked about the need to have rigor around doing what they said they were going to do during the meeting. An easy practice, that would make a big difference, was simply keeping a record of decisions made at the meeting, including next action steps (who, what, and by when). At the end of meeting we would review the notes so that there was little chance of confusion or misunderstanding or forgetting what was promised. The CEO endorsed this with a strong, affirmative statement; "We have to do this!" There followed a collective nodding of heads.

As we approached the end of the meeting and everyone were closing their computers and getting ready to go, we said, "Okay, let's review the decisions and the action steps." They kept moving, saying, "Nah, we don't have to do that – we got it", and left the conference room. The CEO, stunned, said, "I guess we have our work cut out for us."

After years of consulting to senior executives and upper level managers on execution management systems, we have concluded *there is extraordinary resistance from individuals and organizations to addressing and getting better at execution.* As logical and beneficial that improving execution has been proven to be, not everybody embraces it and many out-and-out fiercely resist.

When discussing with executives how execution practices can be learned and applied, some say things like; "We already do something close enough to that," "We're pretty good at execution," "We're too busy," "The time's not right," "I can't ask my people to do one more thing," "We tried something like that and it didn't work," "We're not disciplined enough to do that" or "It'll never fly here." And for those who do get it and have even brought an execution management system into their organization, they often run into some significant hurdles to implementing it along the way. A hurdle, of course, is something you have to jump over in order to reach the finish line, or, according to the dictionary, it's a problem you must solve or deal with before you can make progress. One important step to dealing with the hurdles to execution is to know what forms of resistance you can anticipate – both your own as well as others in your organization.

What follows is geared toward organizations taking on improving execution. If you're not a leader in an organization and want to take on improving your ability to execute, you still want to be aware that people around you may be affected by some of these same hurdles as well.

The hurdles are not insurmountable. You just need to know about them in order to better ensure that you won't be stopped by any of them.

**The Forms of Resistance (Hurdles):**

**Hurdle #1: Until people discovers execution for themselves, they really don't see the value of it.**

As we have been discussing all along, you have to discover execution as something real and with substance before you'll have any desire to work on it. You have to see and envision the value.

**Hurdle #2: People who have never been held accountable for results are terrified of the idea of it.**

This means almost everybody. Most people have been given accountability for *activities* or to oversee activities and that's different than accountability for *results*. When you're accountable for results it means you have to *deliver*. If you don't, you're failing at your job and there are consequences, real or perceived. Only a small percentage of people who comprise the workforce have ever had this kind of accountability (mostly it's commissioned sales people as well as some entrepreneurs).

The fear of being held accountable can be very strong and often not conscious. It's a mistake to underestimate the overwhelming power of terror – your own or that of others. Beyond a shadow of a doubt, underneath the relatively confidant exterior, when it comes to accountability, there's terror. Anybody who has worked in a large enough organization has probably heard some version of the speech that includes; "…So from now on we're going to hold everyone accountable for doing what their job requires and to the degree it is required. We will all have goals and we all will be expected to meet them." To keep the terror under control, staff will nonchalantly sigh and often say silently, "This, too, shall pass." Most are just hoping this won't change anything.

Another ploy is to go to the leader that is standing for having a culture of accountability and tell him or her why this is a bad idea. It's not because they are bad people or conscious saboteurs; it's that they're scared.

The fear is that we'll fail, or that life as we know it is changing and it's going to be hard and uncomfortable. However, accountability/being held accountable is not the boogie man. Most people, who have enough experience at being held accountable for results, will tell you that once you've gotten used to it, you'd never go back to the way it was. *The way it was* means when you were guessing whether you were succeeding or not but you never really knew, so you learned to *give the impression* of confidence and competence. Part of what it takes to climb the ladder in a corporate environment is to manipulate the people around you so they will consider you valuable. It's an okay skill, but it's not the same as being someone who can deliver results.

Rather than aspire to get ahead, why not aspire to become someone who knows how to – and is willing to – deliver the desired results. Learning to be that person is not easy at first; it's like learning a new language (and in some ways it *is* learning a new language, the language of execution). The journey to mastery of execution requires that we learn how to deal with people in a useful way when you are faltering or they are not fulfilling their accountabilities. A *useful way* means to not give up when it's you who's struggling. It also means that you don't get angry and punish others when they're struggling. This doesn't mean you back off and fail to hold them accountable. You need to be firm but do it gently. It means you also might need to offer them help. And finally, it means there are consequences for repeated failures to deliver.

**Hurdle #3: People don't keep their promises.**

If you're thinking right now "*I keep my promises,*" you've got a lot of company. Most of us think we do. However, try this challenge: spend the next week being observant of all the promises you make, big and small. This includes all the times you say "I will," or "I'll get that done" or "Okay" to a request because if you say you're going to do something, that counts as a promise. Now, during this challenge, pay attention to how often you didn't follow through on your promises. You'll be surprised by the results.

Most of us believe we're "good" people and we keep our promises. At least that's our intent. The problem is twofold. One is that we believe only "bad" people break their promises. Since we don't want to be bad people, we tend to not notice that we sometimes do break our promises. Two, as long as we believe we always keep our promises, we don't recognize that we don't always do so. And if we don't recognize this, then the chances of our getting better at keeping our promises – doing what we said we'd do – are limited. In other words, you might tell yourself, "Well I keep my promises, so I don't have to get better at it." Yes, you do.

Execution can be said to be nothing more than doing what you said you'd do in the time frame in which you said you'd do it. Getting better at keeping our promises is an essential practice for improvement. We consider it the most basic practice. If you practice keeping your promises, you'll find that you'll be more careful about what you say you'll do. You won't say 'yes' when you can't really promise it. You'll start saying something like "I can promise to attempt to do this, but I have a conflict right now so I can't actually promise I'll be able to get it done." To which you can add: "Is there someone else you can get who can promise this?"

**Hurdle #4: Above all, most people really just want to be comfortable.**

Much of the resistance to change comes from simply not wanting to be bothered by needing to adjust to something new. This resistance is usually reactionary and often blocks the person's willingness to even listen to why the change needs to happen. Even people who tout change for a living (like the authors of this book) often react to even meaningless changes themselves. We like to say, "*To react is human; to recover and re-think is wise.*"

People get used to their jobs; they feel good about what they do and they have a certain routine. Then along comes a manager or an executive who says; "We're going to do things differently around here," and then adds, "We're going to ensure that everybody has measurable goals that they'll be accountable to accomplish." It's a double hit: their world – their stability, their comfortability – and then their very ability to be successful.

Many people at work just wish you'd leave them alone and let them do their job. Many of them will just be quiet about it, hoping it'll all just go away. We need to take this into account in our change initiatives, in our plans on transforming our organizations into high performance ones – ones that are willing to master execution.


## Hurdle #5: The organizational drift is built on avoiding discomfort.

If you shy away from using the word *culture*, as in "corporate culture", and look for what's actually happening in organizations without the bias that goes with that word, some interesting things open up as possibilities. What most people call *culture* we call *the drift.* If you go to a river and float on your back in the drift, guess in which direction your body will move? It's the same with an organization – they all have their own drift, the direction everything is going. It's "how things work around here."

The tendency in most organizations is to keep things as they are, to maintain the status quo. In most organizations the drift is very strong in the direction of "no change here." If you do anything that is going to change things, like implement an execution management system, it helps to know you are "awakening the sleeping dragon" known as the drift, and it'll rear its ugly head and eat your good intentions for breakfast if it can.

**Hurdle #6: The language of execution can be a turn-off.**

Almost all of the words associated with execution have negative connotations in our culture, beginning with the word *execution* itself, which, of course, has another meaning: "chopping off heads." We've already addressed *accountability*, which for many people means "somebody is going to beat me up if I don't do what I was told to do". And a phrase we consider even scarier, *hold other people accountable*, which can mean "if I start calling people on their failure to deliver, they're going to start calling me on mine."

You can add your own words (i.e., promises, stretch goals, discipline, responsibility, commitments, etc.) and ask yourself what you might hear when you hear each one. Actually, we don't so much need to change the words; rather, we need to be clear about what we mean when we use them. We need to re-define them in the context of getting better at execution, of accomplishing our vision, our mission, our initiatives and our goals.

**Hurdle #7: Lack of courage and commitment on the part of the senior executive.**

This is a biggie. It's not only a hurdle, it also holds the key to being successful at getting others to be part of the early stages of an organizational commitment to execution, and to be willing to stay the course. Without strong leadership, it's not going to happen. Strong leadership must start at the top and then trickle down. Everyone in a leadership position needs to step up to the plate.

What we mean by *strong leadership* is that sometimes a leader has to be willing to make a decision and then stand his or her ground throughout the period of change or growth. We've found quite often, when discussing the possibility of taking on getting better at execution with an organizational leader, they sometimes want to "run it by their team" first, before they make a decision. While we salute the desire to include the team in important decisions, sometimes you can't do that, and this is one of those times. If you do "run it by your team" first, the odds are you're going to end up saying "No", because at least some people on your team will want to squelch it (for the reasons we've said in this chapter), and you won't move forward.

You've got to be able to say, "We are going to do this." Or, later, "We are doing this." You have to be steadfast. It is times like these that what it means to be a leader is tested. It is tests like these that build strong leaders.

**Summary**

If taking on getting better at execution and being on the journey to mastery of execution was easy and obvious, everybody would be doing it. There's tremendous resistance in organizations to change, and especially so when that change involves concepts that seem to be a threat to employees' comfort and ultimately their very jobs.

We've broken down the resistance into what we call hurdles. As a senior leader you have to first and foremost find the strength of conviction to even get started. We, who have coached executives and managers in taking on execution in their organization, know that a leader's lack of strength will always kill real change. Once you start, it helps to know the resistance is there. If you don't, you'll run into resistance that you won't even see coming. If you know these hurdles are at work, you'll move more skillfully through them (or over them) and you're more likely to succeed, and to stay the course.

*You will succeed if you persist. You will accomplish great things.*

# NOTES

# NOTES

# Chapter 9

# Okay, So Now What?

*"Twenty years from now you will be more disappointed by the things you didn't do than by the ones you did do. So throw off the bowlines. Sail away from the safe harbor. Catch the trade winds in your sails. Explore. Dream. Discover."*

Mark Twain

You've read this far and you're almost to the end of the book. We have no way to know what it's been like for you – what your adventure into discovery has been so far. In the previous chapter we discussed the resistance to execution and it's quite likely there's been resistance to some of what we're expressing regarding the journey to mastery of execution. There's a myriad of possible forms your journey has taken: enjoyment, frustration, wrestling to understand, lights going on in your head, mild to heavy disagreement, wondering how to apply any of it to your life or to your organization, laughter, fear, regret, boredom, and so on. Welcome then, to your own journey. Take a look at the cover picture again, the rickety bridge, and rejoice that you've made it to this place.

*So now what?*

If we've been successful, you have at least some interest in testing the waters. Some of you have already been trying out some of what we've outlined here. Others of you have been waiting to see – your inner jury is still out.

**Recommended Steps**

What we intend to do now is help you have some direction from here. Action is required. You can draw your own map, but we'd like to contribute to your thinking about what that map might look like.

Chapters 1 through 8 dealt with some of the essential elements on the journey to mastery of execution. We put those chapters into the order we thought would be the most logical for understanding, not necessarily in the order of being the most logical for action. By essential, we mean *if you don't include these elements, you'll not get far on your journey until you do.* By *elements,* we mean them to be considered in the context of the "science" of execution that we illustrated in chapter three. The *atom* is the dual unit of requests/promises: the *molecule* is the execution cycle; and the *elements* include what is referred to in each of the chapters. There are more elements that we didn't go into here and there are even more that we haven't discovered yet.

At this point in your journey, it's time to re-consider chapter 5 on commitments. It's time to take that first step of committing yourself to action. It could be a commitment to move forward, to take the next step or steps that will be an expression of commitment and will put something at stake. Here are a few possibilities:

As an individual, commit to:

- discovering execution (if you haven't already)

- the practice of keeping your promises

- the practice of using the execution cycle

- treating your relationships at work as if they really matter

- developing and using your own language of execution

- learning how to manage execution

As a senior leader, commit to:

- the suggestions for the individual listed above

- sharing the book with others in your organization – then discussing it together

- the fulfillment of your key goals/initiatives for the year

- implementing an execution management system

- hiring a consultant/coach that can guide you on the journey

These are suggestions for getting started. As we said in chapter 7, every journey begins with the first step and the first step to the mastery of execution is to make the commitment to it. This means you start learning and practicing the essential elements of execution. When you reach a point in which you're ready to be fully committed to the journey, then make the full commitment. And most importantly – *stick to it!*

## The Elements Ordered by First Things First

This is not meant to be a strict guideline on what to do in what order. It's meant to be an example of a map with some suggestions so you can do what makes sense for you. We recommend re-reading the chapters as you begin to integrate them into your practices.

### 1. Commitment

Commit to something to get started – something that's not so easy for you to do but represents that you're serious about moving forward. Keep in mind that nothing extraordinary ever was accomplished without commitment. Whatever you commit to accomplish, make it something that would be big for you. Something you would feel really good about accomplishing.

Take advantage of whatever the time of year it is right now. For example, if it's September, you might want to commit for the period that is left in the year. If it's January, then use the year, or if you prefer, make it a half a year. Make it long enough that it's meaningful for you, but not so long that it may tend to lose its meaning. If it's November, make it to the end of next year, or mid-next year.

At the very least, commit to whatever three to five key results or initiatives are most important to you for this period of time. You may want to start the list by asking "What do I have to accomplish this year?" or "What do I want to accomplish this year?" but when you commit, they become "What I am declaring I will do this year." You have transformed a "should" or a "want" to a "will!" This is a very good beginning.

Commitments are not articulated once and then forgotten. Once committed, you're fully committed and your actions will include reminding yourself of your commitments as often as you need. When you find yourself relaxing on a commitment, doing or not doing something that is taking away from that accomplishment, re-declare what you're committed to.

There's a saying: *"You can never be fully committed sometimes."*

107

This first step not only confirms where you intend to go, it also is a way to practice the art of being committed.

## 2. Discovering Execution

It is arguable whether *commitment* comes first or *discovering execution* comes first. You probably won't commit to execution without discovering it first; but it's unlikely that your discovery of execution will occur without committing to it. If you like, you can make the 2nd step the 1st. Maybe they would best be coupled together.

Whatever the order, you'll not get far if you haven't discovered execution for yourself. How would you know if you did?

Here are some signs that you haven't:

- You don't know what the fuss is all about. You've been executing all of your adult life.

- You're perfectly satisfied with the way things are. You don't accomplish much but you consider yourself good at what you do.

- You thought the book was interesting, but you didn't try any of the suggested actions (for example, you didn't observe yourself promising for a week).

- Here are some signs that you have discovered execution:

- You see the possibilities and you're eager to get going.

- You're banging your forehead because you can't believe you haven't realized any of this until now.

- You're excited about the future, when your level of ability to execute or your company's level of ability to execute is greatly improved.

You may or may not be 100% sure, but you're ready and raring to go. If you're in that place, just moving forward will bring your discovery into clearer focus. One thing you could do is re-read chapter 1 again – "What Is Execution?" A practice you could take on is being aware of when you see good execution around you and also when you see poor execution around you. In other words, be discerning about execution.

### 3.  The Language of Execution

This is more of an organizational element than an individual one, because it's mostly relevant when working together with groups of people. Any company of any size needs to take this on, which basically means there needs to be a re-thinking and a re-stating of the most common words we use in executing. Again, re-read chapter 2 to get some ideas of what this means and how to go about it.

In particular, not considering and giving this topic its due could kill off any attempt to change an organization from one that is at best, haphazard in execution, to one that's masterful in it. If co-workers are disenchanted with the words you use, they will not hear your message.

Our recommendation is for you to do just what we did in chapter 2. We listed the main words used, asked around and found out what those words often mean to people. Then we made it our business to re-define the words and whenever we used them, we repeated what we meant by them, until we could sense when the new meaning was being embraced. By doing this, you'll make good progress in terms of the expectations in your organization regarding commitment, results, and accountability.

### 4. The Resistance

These first four elements comprise what might be considered the foundation elements since they need to be started early on and continued because everything else can be said to stand on their solidity. You can never forget that there's an apparently natural resistance to many aspects of execution, for all of the reasons we said in chapter 8.

You have to know that there are people who will be resistant in the beginning. Of those who resist, some will quickly see that it's easier to do it than to resist it. They'll think, maybe it isn't so bad, anyway. However, there are going to be people who will fight it forever, and you'll want to set it up so that the die-hard resisters end up going somewhere else. Meanwhile, you and your organization of deliverers will be soaring.

If you're a leader in an organization, we highly recommend that you set it up so that people understand that the expectation is that *every person here is expected to be successful at their job.* Although there should be a lot of room to have learning periods where people can become successful at their job, there has to be a point, that if their job is not getting done, the company will need to give someone else the opportunity to be successful at it. You also set it up so that managers understand that they're there to support the people they manage in being successful. The managers will be successful when their direct reports are successful.

You don't need to fight resistance with equal and opposite resistance. This is not the kind of workplace anyone would want. Rather, you give the energy of resistance some room to stop being oppositional and start working in favor of the success of your enterprise. This does not mean you give in to it; it means you give it time to transform as you insist on the expectations you have of your people.

One thing to remember is that whenever you hire someone new in your organization you're going to have to integrate them into your culture. They need to know early on that if they take the job, they're going to be expected to be successful at it. This is the best introduction you can give to get them going in a good direction right away.

## 5. The Execution Cycle

Practicing the execution cycle – requests, promises, and follow up – is a basic practice for getting better at execution, and needs to be practiced by everyone in an organization. Once you learn it, you'll be able to teach it, and you'll need to. This way, everyone in the company will become familiar with how to get work done.

Re-read chapter 3. There's a lot more to the cycle than we could put into one chapter, but the basic practice can be applied over and over, many times a day, and the return will be great. You will be getting what you wanted when you wanted it, and the people around you will be practicing being accountable and being deliverers.

Just doing this one practice will transform your workplace. Do it and keep doing it. You'll be amazed at what you'll accomplish.

We've mentioned this before, but just as a caution: If you turn this into a weapon to use against people or to be better than others, it'll work against you. We like to think that organizations that get good at this turn into arenas of harmonizing choirs of people working together. While those that don't use it, are just merely gawky noisemakers.

Shakespeare describes it best:

*"It is a tale told by an idiot, full of sound and fury, signifying nothing."*

## 6. Relationships

Giving *relationships* a separate slot in a list of the elements of execution mastery is almost like separating breathing from going about your day-to-day activities. Everything we've been discussing here has to do with relationships and relationships are ultimately what working together with others is all about.

Still, as we mentioned in chapter 4, even though it's almost universally agreed to be the essential ingredient in organizational execution, almost nobody has any practices or any special attention on their relationships at work.

The good news is you can change this in *your own workplace* by taking on some practices that will enhance your work relationships. Keep in mind, the purpose of your relationships at work is to enhance the success of the enterprise. Your job is to enable and unleash the power of relationships by giving them the attention they deserve.

The most basic practice is to remember why you're there together – to forward the progress of the organization. You do that every day in every encounter with others; or, you don't. It's your choice. Are you going to nurture your working relationships with people around you, or are you going to avoid people, or avoid conflict; or wrestle with them over who has the power; or threaten them in some way, or order them around; and so on? Every time you encounter another, remind yourself: *I am here to help them help the company be successful.*

Another practice is to be mindful of how you talk to people and to shift your orientation to the purpose of your relationships – all day, every day. Pay attention to your relationships, as much as you can. Be the reminder for others to remember why they are there. Pay them the honor of making requests of them, of listening to their promises in response to those requests, and following up to make sure they did what they said they were going to do when they said they were going to do it. Help them be clear when you make requests. Help them learn to be accountable by holding them accountable.

### 7. Managing Execution

Managing execution is another practice for building relationships since both are geared to the same thing – the success of the organization. In fact, all of the elements work together for the same whole entity. Managing execution and building relationships are inter-woven with each other.

One thing to keep in mind is that no "difficult conversation" is all that difficult to have and certainly not worth avoiding at the cost of your organizational ability to execute.

As we expressed in chapter 7, you need a system to manage execution. Adopt a system and commit to it, which includes committing to your own performance objectives. Then let everyone know that the expectation is that they're committed to their own success.

To embrace these elements and put them in action through practices is transformational for your existing enterprise. The good news is that it can and will work, if done right; the bad news is it isn't easy.

## 8. The Journey to Mastery

This is all about mastery, which is always a journey that starts with a first step and has no end. Although the journey to mastery of execution has no end, it does have stages. The stages are such that each one represents a substantial improvement in the ability to execute, and along with that, a substantial improvement in the results in your organization. Our measure is that by staying on the journey, you'll get to a place where you're accomplishing your key initiatives year after year. You've reached a place where you're adept at saying what you're going to do, and, for the most part, accomplish those things. The rewards are enormous.

To get to that place, you must take on the journey. There's plenty of evidence that if you don't, you won't get there. If you don't set your sails for "Ithaka", you'll not get there, says Constance P. Cavafy, in his poem by that name:

*"When you set out for Ithaka ask that your way be long, full of adventure, full of instruction."*

**How It Might Go**

***As an individual***, you can substantially improve your own ability to execute. You'll gain considerably by becoming someone who can deliver results.

How it might go is you make your commitment – say it's that you determine that you're going to dedicate the next six months to practicing both keeping your promises and the execution cycle. These seem to be straightforward practices, but you see that they could be very valuable to you. What you're committing yourself to is the fulfillment of the first phase.

You observe yourself for a week and you realize you promised a number of things that you didn't do and you ended up with some broken promises. Interestingly enough, you found that you made some promises to yourself that you didn't keep. You almost immediately start becoming more thoughtful before you say you'll do something. Your spouse asks you to pull together your business expense receipts so she can do the taxes, and you say, "Sure", and then you realize that was an automatic response to her request and you don't really mean it. You go back and ask her when she needs the receipts, and she says, "I guess by next Monday." In your mind, you calculate how much time it'll take you to gather the receipts and you say, "I'll get them to you first thing Monday morning." You do it, and by the look on her face you surmise that she didn't really expect you to have those receipts at the time you said you would.

At work, you notice that some people tell you what to do and all they expect back from you is an "OK" and then they go about their business. You decide you're not yet going to attempt to apply the execution cycle with them because you weren't ready to be relatively sure you could do it without them thinking there's something wrong with you. Others do actually make it sound like a request, but you're not always sure whether it's meant that way. At first you kind of tippy-toe around this. But soon you start asking for clarification; "When do you want this by?", you ask. "As soon as possible", someone responds. "Will next Friday work for you?" you ask. "That's fine" they say to you. "I'll have it on your desk by next Friday, before closing time", you say. And the execution cycle is in motion.

You continue your practices. You find you're more careful about what you say you'll do. You realize even the demands made at work can be negotiated. You learn to not simply say you'll do something unless you're sure you can. And sometimes you tell people you can't absolutely promise you can get something done but you're willing to take it on with the caveat that if you can't do it, you'll let them know. You write down in a little notebook all of your promises, and you find that even when you promise something you're sure you can do, there are times when you can't or your priorities change and you need to re-promise. You learn to let people know if you can't do what you said you were going to do – and you find out they respect you for that. You are rigorous with the cycles, making sure none are dangling.

You also realize you're training the people around you to expect that you'll make clear promises and that you'll ask questions for clarity when you need to. You realize you're starting to get a reputation for being the "go to" person at work.

At the end of the six months, you feel you've made a lot of progress with these practices and you commit to continuing for another six months. You add to your practices by making goals that are important to you and/or to your company and you commit to them as well.

You may not always be successful at first, but you're on your way. At the end of that second six months, you could be ready to commit to the journey to mastery of execution. "I'm not going to stop at having gotten better at some of it", you say, "I'm ready to take on mastery."

*As a leader or manager*, you'll need to take it on as an individual too. To expect those you lead or manage to do it, you have to do it too. If you don't take it on yourself, at some point your staff begins to see it as management's way to manipulate them to do a better job. If upper management isn't going to do it, it isn't going to go very far with the rest of the organization.

One key to getting your organization to take on improving its ability to execute is for you, the leader, to commit to that improvement and be prepared to lead it. Again, we don't mean you need to commit to the entire journey at this time, but you do need to commit to a serious first year of it. Once you get that year completed -- and if you do it right there'll be gains in that year that will far exceed your investment – you could well be ready to commit to the whole journey.

A second key is *do not try to do this by yourself.* Employ a non-partisan consultant or coach who knows what they're doing and can guide you on your journey and work with you along the way. You're tackling a huge organizational and cultural change – from an organization that is as it is now to one that is moving plan-fully toward being a high performing one. After all, what's a high performing organization but one that year-after-year gets extraordinary results? Think about that. And what is an organization that can be said to have mastered execution? It's one that year-after-year gets extraordinary results. In other words, these two terms are synonymous.

There are very few masters of musical instruments that are self-taught. There are no great athletes who haven't had, or don't have, coaches. Nobody self-teaches and gains a black belt. Moreover, very few companies of any size have successfully transformed themselves without outside help. Why? Because from inside a company all you can do for the most part is make small improvements consistent with the culture you have.

**Summary**

If you've come this far, your journey has begun and you can continue it. We hope you'll continue, and to support your continuing, we gave you some different ways to view your journey from here.

We consider all of the previous chapters to be on topics that comprise the essential elements of the journey to mastery of execution. We recommend starting out with a commitment. As William H. Murray has said in a quote we included earlier: *"Until one is committed, there is hesitancy, the chance to draw back... the moment one definitely commits oneself, then providence moves too."*

We recommend a commitment that has meaning to you. And then stick to that commitment. Actually mean it. And see where that takes you. If you like that early phase of your journey – if you like the results of it – then go on, *because if you always do what you've always done, you'll always be what you are today.*

# NOTES

# NOTES

# A Few Last Words from the Authors

*"Some people go through life trying to find out what the world holds for them only to find out too late that it's what they bring to the world that really counts."*

Lucy Maude Montgomery, author of *Anne of Green Gables*

As we said in the preface, this book is meant to be your vehicle for discovering execution. At the very least we hope it has flipped the switch on the topic of execution for you – from being *unconscious* to *conscious*. Our invitation has been three-fold:

1. We invite you to discover execution.

2. We invite you to learn some practices that will help you improve your individual and organizational ability to execute.

3. We invite you to get on board for the journey to the mastery of execution – the most valuable organizational and personal competency you can have.

*The Age of Execution is upon us! You are welcome to it!*

As best we can, we live our lives conscious of what we're bringing into the world. In this book, we intend to help shepherd into the world of organizations what we see as the Age of Execution. We're delighted about the work we're doing with our clients and the results they're getting. We hope the publication and sales of this book will result in a wider embracing of the concepts and practices presented here.

That being said, we're very grateful that we've had the experience of writing this book. Even though we are individually experienced at writing, our working together has been a joy. We're complementary beings in so many ways. We just seem to have fallen into a methodology in which one drafts content and then together we edit and discuss that content seamlessly. Not because of any personal egotistical needs, but because of the ease and grace of the process and our commitment to the message. We believe this book will be extraordinarily useful and impactful.

In addition, our learning curve about the very topics we've taken on – execution, leadership, relationships at work, and so on – has been much steeper than we could have imagined. We believe our current client base has profited from our revelations, and we know they have greatly contributed to our learning at the same time. We're writing these last few words as a completion of our manuscript, and although we'd love to sell a million copies of the book, we don't need any more recompense than what we've already gained.

We're also grateful to all of the clients we've had over the years, and all of the people who we interacted with, each one of whom has contributed to us. We didn't mention many by name, but you know who you are. And we're grateful as well to so many teachers and mentors and colleagues and even those with whom we have had the most casual of conversations (e.g., on airplanes) that have gone into forming our thinking and our practices. If we tried to list all of the names of those who belong in this category, it would compete with the largest of tomes.

Last but not at all the least, we're grateful to our families for their love and support and especially to our wives who put up with so much sharing of our time and attention in our pursuit of being helpful and earning a place in the world.

Johnny Unitas, who for so long has been considered one of the best quarterbacks in professional American football, said this in 1979 upon being entered into the Football Hall of Fame, and we echo these words:

> *"(One) never gets to this station in life without being helped, aided, shoved, pushed and prodded to do better. I want to be honest with you: The players I played with and the coaches I had ... they are directly responsible for my being here. I want you all to remember that. I always will."*

And as Dale Evans wrote and sang, back in the day, *"Happy trails to you!"*

# About the Kierson Tomlinson Group

*"Learning from the school of hard knocks is very informing, but the tuition is too high!*

*We should learn from other people's experiences."*

Cavett Robert, Founder of the National Speakers Association

We, Miles Kierson and Gary Tomlinson, formed The Kierson Tomlinson Group in order to combine our collective experience and respective capabilities. We did so in service of bringing forth discovering execution and the journey to mastery of execution with a vision of helping organizations go from "good to great." In other words, helping companies become high performance organizations, that consistently achieves their goals year after year.

While in the process of writing this book, we looked at each other and said, "If people need consulting and coaching help in this space, we may be the only ones, at this time, who can do this work as we have been outlining it." Please know this wasn't hubris. What we're saying is that a lot of what you've read here has been discovered and/or developed by us and the other consultancies won't have the expertise in all of these areas at this time.

We're experienced executives ourselves as well as experienced leadership consultants and executive coaches. We're trained, certified and heavily experienced in the KeyneLink execution management system. And we have spent many years helping companies to envision a compelling future, and then help them get there – also known as executing.

**Briefly, here's how we can help**

1. **As speakers and workshop presenters**

   We are nationally recognized professional speakers. Our *"Discovering Execution"* and other execution-related topics serve as a great introduction to the Age of Execution. Whether it's a presentation for an executive team, leadership team or an entire organization our presentations are eye-opening, entertaining, and highly motivating.

Our workshops on executive team alignment and organizational execution are informative, educational, and very interactive. Each one is customized specifically for the client because no two organizations are exactly alike.

We offer a workshop we want to call to your attention because of the impact it has and because of its uniqueness. It's our *Kierson Tomlinson Issues Resolution Workshop*. We have found that organizations often don't resolve their issues; they keep them unresolved – in some cases for years. It has been our experience that with the right forum and the right facilitators you can resolve most issues in a relatively short period of time (we sometimes refer to it as a "locked door" session).

## 2. As consultants

Our unique offering is designed to help organizations take on the journey of learning how to improve their ability to execute in the ways we wrote about in this book and more. Because each client is unique, we customize our process to meet each organization's specific needs. Our coming-in purpose is to get our client on a good track and have them learn and thrive in engaging their organization to improve their ability to produce results. We're specialists in helping develop high performing organizations.

Most often, as part of our offering, we introduce our clients to the KeyneLink execution management system. We help them bring their team into the fold and teach them how to implement this system throughout their organization.

### 3. As executive coaches

Because we're steeped in leadership practices as well as execution practices, we're unique executive coaches. We work with both experienced and new executives as well as high-level managers to help them be better leaders and managers. We help them get over their execution-related hurdles and help them manage their critical relationships – managing both "up" and "down".

### 4. As interim Chief Execution Officer (CXO)

We serve in the capacity of interim Chief Execution Officer (CXO) while we train someone in the organization to take over that function. This is a position we discovered was missing at the C-Suite level, a position that ought to be at least as essential as the other already accepted positions.

The interim CXO's job is to make sure the organization is fulfilling its commitments to its initiatives; that in general everybody is learning to get better and better at execution; that the enterprise is organized to maximize effectiveness; that everyone who is in a management position is utilizing best practices in producing results; that the execution management system is being used to maximize its effectiveness in managing progress and learning; and in general is cultivating a culture of accelerating capability.

There is an old Chinese proverb that says *"The best time to plant a tree was 20 years ago. The second best time is now."* If now is the time for you to get on board, we want to help you.

If you're a CEO, COO, president, or division head of a mid- to large-size company who is interested in pursuing further what we have to offer, we invite you to contact us:

The Kierson Tomlinson Group

www.kiersontomlinson.com

CPSIA information can be obtained
at www.ICGtesting.com
Printed in the USA
LVOW10s1102140617
537816LV00060B/884/P